THE SKIN OF MEANING

THE SKIN OF MEANING

poems

~

Keith Flynn

Red Hen Press | *Pasadena, CA*

Book layout by Wesley Griffith

Library of Congress Cataloging-in-Publication Data

Names: Flynn, Keith, author.
Title: The skin of meaning / Keith Flynn.
Description: First edition. | Pasadena, CA : Red Hen Press, [2020]
Identifiers: LCCN 2019050350 (print) | LCCN 2019050351 (ebook) | ISBN
   9781597098489 (trade paperback) | ISBN 9781597098434 (ebook)
Subjects: LCGFT: Poetry.
Classification: LCC PS3556.L875 S55 2020 (print) | LCC PS3556.L875
   (ebook) | DDC 811/.54—dc23
LC record available at https://lccn.loc.gov/2019050350
LC ebook record available at https://lccn.loc.gov/2019050351

The National Endowment for the Arts, the Los Angeles County Arts Commission, the Ahmanson Foundation, the Dwight Stuart Youth Fund, the Max Factor Family Foundation, the Pasadena Tournament of Roses Foundation, the Pasadena Arts & Culture Commission and the City of Pasadena Cultural Affairs Division, the City of Los Angeles Department of Cultural Affairs, the Audrey & Sydney Irmas Charitable Foundation, the Kinder Morgan Foundation, the Meta & George Rosenberg Foundation, the Allergan Foundation, the Riordan Foundation, Amazon Literary Partnership, and the Mara W. Breech Foundation partially support Red Hen Press.

First Edition
Published by Red Hen Press
www.redhen.org

MIX
Paper from
responsible sources
FSC
www.fsc.org   FSC® C011935

ACKNOWLEDGMENTS

Many thanks to the editors of the following publications in which these poems first appeared:

27 Views of Asheville (anthology), "Et in Arcadia Ego"; *American Journal of Poetry*, "Baby Boomers"; *American Literary Review*, "Caravaggio's Carnal Gospel," "The Agnostic"; *Asheville Citizen-Times*, "Coffin Not Included"; *Best of the Fuquay-Varina Series* (anthology), "A Girl Like That," "This Rock is Gonna Roll"; *Beyond Earth's Edge: The Poetry of Spaceflight* (anthology), "The Invisible Bridge"; *Black Renaissance Noire*, "Gaslight: Inauguration Day," "Look For Me In Liberia," "Louis and The Wolf," "The House of Dance and Feathers" ; *Bluestem*, "The Bookmobile," "Thoughts on Easter While Digging a Grave"; *Cave Wall*, "The Silver Surfer"; *Cimarron Review*, "Blue Mountain Panorama," "*Like A Buddha*, Paul Motian Says," "The Glory Façade" "The Mountain That Eats Men," "Wall Street"; *Colorado Review*, "Le Papillon," "The Exile," "Writer's Block"; *Comstock Review*, "Robert Johnson's *Milk Cow Blues*," "Snow is ghostly . . . ," "The Hidden Life of Ants"; *Confluence: Far From the Centers of Ambition* (anthology), "The Kick of Infinity: Paradoxical Architecture"; *Cutthroat: Truth to Power* (anthology), "Democracy"; *Ecotone*, "The Force of Compassion"; *Enchanted Voices Literary Review* (India), "Nostalgia as Entropy"; *Five Points*, "Glenn Gould in Carnegie Hall, 1962," "*Like a Buddha*, Paul Motian Says"; *The Freeman*, "The Searchers"; *Hampden-Sydney Review*, "Villon"; *Hunger Mountain*, "Stylish Violence"; *Iodine Poetry Journal*, "Prayer," "The Skin of Meaning," "World Boogie"; *James Dickey Review*, "Context," "Dear Reader"; *Minnesota Review*, "Louis and the Wolf"; *North Carolina Conversations*, "The Exile"; *Plume*, "Putting," "The Long Black Road," "Tranquility & Tremolo," "Salvador"; *Poems and Plays*, "Ceremony"; *Poetry East*, "Great Blue Heron"; *Poetry in Plain Sight*, "Great Blue Heron," "Robert Johnson's *Milk Cow Blues*," "Snow is ghostly . . . ," "Why Pluto Is No Longer a Planet"; *Poets Respond to Race* (anthology), "Look for Me in Liberia"; *Portland Review*, "Jack Spicer," "Running with the Bulls"; *Red Truck Review*, "Broken into Light," "Love Among Cannibals"; *Shenandoah*, "Portrait of the Artist as a Spark"; and *Southern Poetry Anthology*, "Nostalgia as Entropy," "The Silver Surfer".

For Denise

the bravest person
I have ever known
whose skin is my own

CONTENTS

ETYMOLOGIES

DICHOTOMIES

NECROLOGIES

THE SKIN OF MEANING

Speech is not dirty silence
Clarified. It is silence made still dirtier.

—Wallace Stevens
The Creations of Sound

ETYMOLOGIES

THE SKIN OF MEANING

He was late to the party and without directions,
though his invitation was secure, and his instincts
keenly honed to an acceptable edge, and as we are
waiting to see if the fates will hear our ode to joy,
we are given the sound of a man losing everything;
this is the hissing of his agitation, the sound of his
broken heart as it is given and fills with shards,
a piece of stone in an overgrown garden, a stiff,
bitter, life-long secrecy tipping over a robust
single indiscretion and no one is witness to the
villain, shaved to a shadow in that moment,
letting the sail of his love loose in a ripping wind
and that lost direction reducing his reflection to
a splinter as he spends his summer cutting down
the grass which grows right back and when the
colder weather comes to drive him down he trims
the fat of his summer words and their loose darkness
swims round his leather chair, the garden vines
emptied of tone, their edges' innuendo snarling,
the hidden realities so carefully furrowed in shy
smiles and feigned deference which fasten his
fading future, slowly shot through with the wrinkles
of original meaning that he has never outgrown.

WHY PLUTO IS NO LONGER A PLANET

for Alan Moore

Of course, my belief
in culture is a sham.
I'm mining this shaft,
nourished on red velvet cake
and scrubbing the live walls
with a ShamWow that
I squeeze for emeralds
like a wizard on holiday.
Don't ask me to explain.
It would only force you
to turn on a television.

There is an outcropping,
a bitter pill hanging onto
the cliff of the universe
like an old icy tooth.
It tastes of burlesque and
Aqua Velva, soft shoe
routines and bent spoons, went
the way of the Andromeda Strain.
Imagine an unnamed finger
grew out of the heel
of your hand and froze there.

ET IN ARCADIA EGO

When the trees bow
and bushes curtsy, as
the silk wind brushes
through my bramble-
cluttered garden, the
claws of the field mice
and piston-powered
rabbits scramble the
unbroken dirt, the
untended roses groan
under the weight of
their thorns, the
untethered tomato vines
sprawl and dump their
fire-red loads among
the robust weeds.
At one corner, Japanese
hornets have assembled
a gray colony the size
of a watermelon and
ward off semi-serious
excursions to pluck
a renegade bud or
puckered potato already
on the verge of rot.
A toxic black walnut
tree stands sentinel
at the leaning gate,
dropping its dark
grenades into the field's

jumbled stalks. Two
squirrels quarrel over
which one should
command this wasted
circle first, the entire
acre fat on my neglect.

THE FORCE OF COMPASSION

Sit with things and listen long
and the singing will begin.
Turn your free fall into
a voluntary act. The song
shattered, every being
takes its piece of the harmony.
The well of the past is bottomless
and in the walls the song climbs
out of the nets and jewels of time,
the infinite unraveling mingled
with bitter intervals of radiance,
well water, lotus heart, rising crane.

THE HOUSE OF DANCE AND FEATHERS

You got to roll with it, or else you'll roll
under it, says the piano player, roiling
the air with arpeggios. The genius is in
the second line, the one entranced and
in thrall to the drum, where the fierceness
of the soil is made manifest, its black mass
loosened by the rhythm of the water roots.

If Heaven is the place where nothing ever
happens, then the stomp and pomp takes
place elsewhere. Horses fear bridges
because of their binocular vision. Unable
to see straight in front of them, their
survival instincts have fashioned a 180
degree panorama in their peripheral scope,

with two realities constantly in play, like
the whale heads hanging on either side
of the Pequod's stern, whom Melville
named Kant and Locke; our perception
is only narrowed when our brain feels
threatened. In Antelope Canyon, on
Navajo Land, Heaven is slotted in

the sandstone, and gossamer beams
of light compete with the waterfalls
to frame a vision of life after death.
The Crack and the Corkscrew spiral
out of the layered earth tones like a
pair of Dante's hellish circles, where
painters and mathematicians spar with

sediment for the symmetrical spoils,
though sometimes the occasional flash
flood will claim a tourist or two.
In Heaven, to whom does one confess?
And when does Death show his face?
Perhaps there the water is made of silk,
and the substance washing around you

is called Grace. Seven white coroner's
sheets covered seven unarmed black
men, who were killed by white police
this week in America, and each of the
deceased's mother or wife believed
their beloved was in a Gucci stall being
fitted for wings. Every policemen thinks,

there but for the Grace of God go I.
Does the Governor of Heaven care about
the color of the murderers? Is there a
great slide, shaped like a bell curve, that
drops the unworthy straight into Hell?
Or streets paved with gold, diamond
Jacob's Ladders, leading the freshly

christened cherubs on escalators into
the segregated first class seats?
On Earth as it is in Heaven, says the
solemn congregation, where the lion
lives in harmony with the lamb.
Awake for five straight days, eating
speed and drinking tequila, Mickey

Newbury swore to me that he'd
seen Jesus, and how did he know?
Had to be Him, said Mickey, He had
on an eggshell robe with the letters JC
monogrammed on the breast pocket.
When 4-year-old Colton Burpo told his
father, Pastor Todd, that he had visited

Heaven while having his appendix
removed, he had sat in JC's lap and
summoned angels with halos riding
rainbow horses and singing his favorite
song, dressed to the nines, with fashionable
robes and purple sashes, and best of all,
no lines for the rollercoasters. Trayvon

Martin's parents said their slain son was
in Heaven with God, and was wearing his
hoodie. Plato's assertions put the temporal
body in peril, but the immortal soul could
eventually have a conversation with anyone.
The pagans thought the soul just stewed,
until the Captain of the New Groove Ship

descended from Heaven and united every
saved soul, dead or alive, under one cool
banner, and cast out old Scratch, and put
out that Lake of Fire, just as soon as the
wicked were tossed in, and then it was
fireworks and roasted hot dogs for all
eternity. But what if this is it? This one

wild life, on a single blue pebble, caught
in a vast webbing of dimensions? I take
no pleasure in the capricious exclusion
of any known Heaven. I spent my child-
hood asking forgiveness of a father who
did not exist, and could not listen, a myth
in the settled universe whose conjuring

only adds to the random strangeness
of humans, now clearly standing in the
margins of their own demise, faced with
the unyielding despair and certainty that
this galaxy must end in ruin, with our
species scattered among the celestial
debris. I cannot fault any being that

seeks a balm in some perfect afterlife's
Wonderland, though the nature of their
prosperity gospel means one man's
salvation is achieved upon the broken
back of his neighbor. The soul's habitation,
should it exist, leads to the imagination's
redemptive force. We are what we make,

and the making is love, and love is the
mystery that sustains us. Any tacit
acknowledgement of religion's cheap
tricks opens the vistas of the unknown.
The higher we climb, the world lays
wider in our scope. The more I know,
the less certain I am, and my self-

deception grows commensurate with
my ignorance. What we have is here,
where we are is now, in Time's despicable,
multi-tentacled clutches, in the habitat
of dance and feathers, building our
headdress and staking our territory,
lending our love's disguise to the march.

PRAYER

Red spruce trees
that yield
their wood
for the violins
made in
Cremona Italy
grow in the same
valley and have
done so since the
1500s including
the Stradivarius
tables and arms
that produce
the sweetest sounds
known to man
650 or so
instruments
worth millions
played by students
in worship of a tone
they cannot
reproduce
any other way
A single man
stands
fingering the strings
in the Dolemites

among
the reverent limbs
of the lovely spruce
making a song
that the wood
can recognize
as the new violins
are forming
in the ageless
swaying trunks

THE GLORY FAÇADE

No one gets the life they deserve.

Eternity is not the endless passage
of time, uninterrupted.
It is contained in a single moment,
where time has stopped,
a frozen moat,
a conversation with a stone.

Each year a column, slowly tilting.
"God is the only architect,"
sd. Gaudi. "I merely copy."
He became a studious imitator
of the tree, the river, the wind.

Light builds everything,
strings of light
torn from sheer blocks,
streamers inviting you
to reconnect them;
the tails of comets,
the rocket's smoky trail
mixed among vaporous clouds,
mist off a boiling pot,
the searching vine's restless rivulets.

Gaudi was killed by a streetcar,
seditiously moored to its tracks,
unable to pass through him,
or follow his immense light.

Buildings are made of music,
            rising with purpose,
filling the air's geometry with forms.
Cities should be built
from the worship
            of nothing in particular,
        and filled with the feelings
    of its people, the only mortar
        that can reinforce the beams.

From this I make my life a bell
and hurl its chime
                across the expanse,
        and a gong of years develops,
buttressed by nothing.

The spool of that life
is filled with temporary commotions,
        knowing that a human being
            in love with mystery
                is never finished

THE EXILE

This is my last letter. The first one
disappointed in a love triangle has
lost the game. Some things upon
which I've aimed were undoubtedly
innocent; but that is for others to decide.
I've tried to rope the world in countless
ways and have done the best I can,
with tangled prayers and no reprieve.
The danger in the Beast is its seasons.

The morning star enlightened Buddha
and his first words formed a poem
out of the desperate ardors,
adders made of words, blind as a boxer,
striking out at every sound.
How do we discriminate?
The map is linear, but poetry is
circular and continuous,
untangling as it tells.

THE BOOKMOBILE

for Kay Ryan

Here comes that tinny bookmobile
and the children whinny and giggle,
their mouths in the shape of a comb,
a gaggle who open books and find
an ice cream cone is waiting, in icy
repose, just resting there in the gutter,
and when the children butterlick the
cone down flat their tongues turn
black and swell so big that they won't
fit back and poems form on them.

RETAIL

I will make my art in the margin, I said,
while everyone scurries to look busy,
hoping to impress the Boss,
whose business is failing,
and now must lay his employees off.

I don't move a muscle,
hamstrung by commission,
and naturally gifted with gab.
I'm used to leaving a big impression

and saying little, my position
secure, having outlasted my peers
who swam back to the university
to spawn their books, whose years

are filled with glib rejoinders
to colleagues about tenure and
pension plans, summers at Yaddo
and Vermont, the right density of manure

for their organic gardens. Fearless,
I will build a church of good-byes,
poems that work their retail magic
even on holidays, that wink when
they should wallow, and kneel for no man.

PUTTING

for John Groover

It's easy to get the yips.
Any small ration of anxiety
will set the hands a-flutter.
Forget the hypnosis and
meditation techniques,
focus instead on the hole,

that Freudian objective,
staring with its bad eye,
out of a perfectly manicured
jigsaw puzzle of jumbled
green elements, designed
to humble every human
who stares intently into it.

In this drama, light reverses
itself and doubt is born.
The first sob does not grate,
but makes all intoxication rise,
doom-eager, as the eagles
of blackness band and lower
their fierce, unyielding beaks.

This is the path to creation,
the dark dive, the arrow
of the mind that screams
for oblivion, even as the
handle in your hands turns
into a crossbow that cannot
find its tricky target among

the endless surprises of sand
and water and hungry stalks
of untrammeled grass. First
thing to go are the eyes and
then the distance shimmies
and one imagines whole towns
sawed apart by the tornado's

tip, as the finger of God
touched down and the white
ball becomes an iris, a star,
a twinkle in the drain that
might guide this sparkle
of luck, this forty foot

birdie putt, this clown mouth
hoping to regain its
clumsy, clueless tooth,
laughing its black one-liners
as the dimpled orb lips
round its warm pocket
and winnows happily out.

CONTEXT

With great risk comes greater risk
and to live in the inquiry is to abandon
the safe proximity of childish expectation.
Be careful, my father says, at every parting,
as if he remembered the lesson of Cicero,
though he does not, whose head was separated
from its body politic and raised on a pike,
after a lady, not a lover, stuck a pin
through his tongue with a sign that foretold
the editorial. *Enough of his eloquence,* the
message read, and one would have to possess
the brain of a chickpea not to get its point.
Context is a faith that cuts both ways,
a perfectly fitted gown, and the greatest gift,
even among the gods, is the suave, authentic
remnant of silent knowing, the arched eyebrow,
the well-placed wink, bereft of seductive
diffidence, beaten clean of detached ambivalence,
robust with plenty in reserve, dense with sly
experience, and remarkably, all in—

NOSTALGIA AS ENTROPY

*If, before the Bang, there was nothing, and if all energy since then
is expended in the manner best suited to return the world to that state,
then all seemingly random permutations of energy dispersal must be
attempts to accelerate the return to chaos.* —David Mamet

The entire universe, the size of a marble,
exploded and is still expanding,
water moving from high energy to low,
seeks the bottom, and every being follows it.

Lincoln believed that all nations must shed
their energy, and that wealth accrued from
slavery would be dispersed through war,
downstream from the dreams of the Constitution.

True human nature is dissipation, the release
of stored light into chaos. The good old bad
old days are always in the past, blockading Cuba,
or bombing Nagasaki, humans joined at the neck

with machines. The rule book of diffusion directs
us to make treaties with the Native Americans,
because to live like Falstaff requires tremendous
amounts of fuel. Entropy never sneezes, does not

like magic or crocodiles or penicillin, hiccups only
if the planets stop orbiting around their Sun.
We want our designs to articulate a meaning
beyond function. We want to own an experience

we have not felt, just as Foucault wanted to turn
his life into a work of art. We embrace the guilt,
and arrange our chips in a manner that will affect
the outcome of the football game. We accept

the superstition's fetish and believe by eating
the organic apple, and stacking the plastic bottles,
we will hold back the erosion of the glaciers.
We tell ourselves we're doing our part and keep

our fair practice good coffee karma intact.
The Starbucks logo features a double-tailed
mermaid that is swimming in neither direction.
The enlightened consumer is in pursuit of happiness,

hedonism disguised as spiritual freedom, paradise
purchased one cup of coffee at a time, like a bird
repeatedly attacking its reflection on the window.
Not the thing itself, but the representation.

Coca-Cola was a tonic, but Coke is iconic,
a brand inseparable from our cultural experience,
like a print taken from a finger, lingering less.
Let's forget, for a second, the syrupy effervescence,

or the grand imitations, Pepsi, Pepper, Pibb.
Just as we do not practice the pronouncement
of our neighbor's names; we know them by their Prius.
Our language is alive and cannot designate reality,

but becomes a beacon, or signal, of our relation,
ghost isotopes that build a memory from the alphabet
and provide a trail for the sale, like the mystery
of Coke, the more you drink, the more you want.

Some stars catching our worried gaze have
already ceased to exist, so far away only their light
is left, disappearing in the cold static space.
Those quiet mornings alone, or in fading twilight,

when the mind wanders backward on its tracks,
cirrus clouds thinning on the scarred horizon,
dolphins plowing together in the near surf,
or insects chirring atop the gently trembling trees,

each given significance as markers for a life.
A bone-encased pocketknife, peacock earrings,
an uncle's dragon scarf folded out of Saigon's
final chaos, slowly lose their luster, or complicated

memory, as the generations stand at attention
in the roll call of deplorable time.
The clusters of music, whose muscles cannot
outlast the marathon of styles, are layered

era upon era, sparkling melodies recycled
by attentive geologists digging through
the stacked boxes in the attic or the basement.
Let the wan night, even when wintered,

fight the gauze of nostalgia and give refuge
to every fire, the future freshened,
and hard run sharpened against
the only path found, signpost labeled

what is to come, what is to come, what is to come.
If it takes the lives of twelve bees to make
a teaspoon of honey, why is it so absurd to believe
that our bodies are composed entirely of light?

GREAT BLUE HERON

for Amanda

Unable to extricate
itself from the silver
     flash of trout
the spirit of the river
the great blue heron
     its head shaped
like a rock hammer
stalks the brooking edge
     on spindly stilts
and braids his hunger
into the oncoming
     and infinite curl
of brisk mountain water
before the twin flames
     of wings spread
without warning
and lifts the whole
     giant jumble of sticks
and feathers silently
into a blue javelin
     cruising upon
the jagged silver currents
     of the sky

MONTAUK

The hicks circling seaward
between Lazy Point and the Goffs,
sturdy stock whose forefathers
ordered the beheading

of Charles I, and thereafter
fled to the Napeague Isthmus,
a promised land of littoral
drift looking down on the

goats grazing in Elisha's Valley.
Poor Elisha, the last of the
Montuketts to rage against
the sailing machines. He said

he would try to forgive the trees
their majesty and helped shear
the mountain knoll bald
at the turn of the century.

When we become what we
are running from, we will
circle where we walk
like a drunken hawk.

DEMOCRACY

The President is so still the people can hear the planets
scraping through space like a fork on a plate.
In their little closets, draped in black flags, the voting hands
grip the iron ball of the one-armed bandit,
listening to the jingle jangle gamble of the capitalist machinery.

Like mercury unable to be trapped beneath your thumb,
the numb citizen, facing that horrible mirror of election,
sees every constituency's refracted self-interest reflected but their own.
When the people stop to consider their choices
they are like clews of worms beneath the ground so busy
that the Senators can feel the earth moving the walls of their Coliseum.

We assign a day and the soul's lead filaments scatter to its magnet.
More women commit suicide on Mother's Day, for instance,
and Black History Month loosens the racist tongues.
The prostitute is a book of knowledge, says the cop
and wakes every morning with a yes on her mind,
drawing to her the nefarious elements.

In the late nineteenth century you could see the hats holding men
by their heads against the ground. Great Lakes Indians
knew their enemies would be coming soon
when the honeybees preceded them. European flies, the Natives
called when they pointed at the regular black clouds as Columbus
restored Pangaea and viruses stormed out of the ship's hold.

The founding fathers, in their powdered wigs, could not
have conceived of satellites or cyberspace, and politely believed
that the citizens would become as one, so thankful for their freedom
from tyranny, that if given a choice, they would always commiserate
and that the deathly grave and greedy glance would give way

to the love of country, and though comprised of a thousand
darkened guesses, the Patriot would rush from shadow to shadow
until he embraced and held the one that housed Salvation,
and patiently wait until the ocean was frozen in place, and time
had mended its savage mandate, which lo and behold, all along
had been focused on a bandage, on the far side of the moon,

a true Super Bowl, where the people in a wave are brushing
and braiding the frayed rope ends of their broken and scattered
commitments, guessing at what new form awaits them
on the opposite humming shore, while below in the Coliseum
playground, the Senators have formed a single block
and cannot be moved, entangled like dogs in heat.

Their interns take turns throwing water on the heap of suits,
but they have come to resemble in their spectacle, a giant log
approaching a waterfall, fixed in its course upon a raging river
and covered in swarming teams of black and silent ants,
all of them calmly refusing to communicate, ignoring the roar
beyond their barge, each convinced they are the one in charge.

CLINTON REDUX

Two decades later and I don't look so bad.
I sorta felt that way about women, from 40 yards
away, they're all beautiful; but you know I was
just a few pregnant chads from hanging around
anyway, and our second black president looks
a little spooked in these headlights. Hanging,
swinging or dimpled, it's a dogfight for the scraps,
and shit, look at Al, he's got his own issue
to wrestle with. He just seemed so natural
playing second fiddle, and he can fight the
bejesus out of Global Warming, bigger discovery
for him than the Internet. I've been this way so
long, I've forgotten how it started, sparked by
a minor annoyance and built indiscretion
by innuendo into a silent loathsome simmer.
If they didn't need me so bad, I wouldn't have
to drag back and forth, but I know how to pump
up the gate. You work so hard, she says; you
deserve better. But I am unable to move both
ways, trapped and confused, I pace between
black suits. The long mad sea of eyes is frozen
into wax; and I am nauseated and exalted, my
arms pedal in greeting like a wood duck's legs
laving in a flood. The tiresome mass of well-
wishers roped in cascading stares, their arms
rippling out. But all habits are bad, Hell,
everybody ought to ride on somebody's
shoulders just once. The American symphony
is intermingled with retribution. I only lost
one election, and I vowed never again to take it,

just sit and take it. You got to respond to their hits
immediately and push back harder. Nothing like
a good old political dogfight to put the roses
in your cheeks. Nobody loved it more, well,
maybe Roosevelt, but he needed it more than me.
But I still get chills when I enter the Oval Office;
and I'm disoriented easily on this side of the desk.

WALL STREET

The square rows of empty buildings
look more
like the rumor of a freckled town,
a faint mirage
that a city had once existed in these
flat margins,
a myth, a whiff, rather than the real
shoulders
of a potent hamlet for the youngsters
to stand upon.

I just try not to smile at strangers anymore,
she says, I want
to save the collagen that's left in my face.
In these locked
rooms, we dream the wings that make a
human seem
holier than the things he builds and abandons,
that a man
is more grand than a humpback or giraffe.
At what point

do the bad men begin to resemble one another,
when the prison
and the prisoner cannot be ascertained, and
becomes a museum,
with flesh-filled artifacts, made entirely of
geometry and fire?
What expectation of divine reward makes
Sunday morning

the most segregated day in America?
And what invisible
boundary makes everyone stay on their side?
Our fledgling
country, drunk on its first taste of universal
sovereignty, sees
in its history an infinite series of svelte hyphens,
connecting traces
of a freedom filled with uncertainty, flailing
in religious halls,
with famous salesmen's portraits hanging on the walls.

CLIMATE CHANGE

If you want to know
what God thinks about
Wealth, then closely
observe the people
She decides to give it to.

Down in the depths of the
90th floor, porters wrap
the mistresses in poised pink
bows, keeping the ginger tea
steeped and hot, micromanaging

the dust on the well-hung
Basquiat. Hand grenades,
disguised as forget-me-nots,
while away the time in gold
and jade pots, close to the

button that opens the well-
appointed panic room.
In the street, the poor fight
to the death for the hand-me-
downs and shave themselves

to fit in the slits of sunshine
filtering between the tower's
blackened mirrors. What good
is living if you can't design
your own scent, from the

squeezed glands of civets
and rare orchid petals, or to
have your loafers sewn
from the pelt of the latest
endangered animal, with

thread comprised of a truly
precious metal? What could
be more slick than a necklace
made of scorpions, and to
wear it properly you only

have to remain completely
still? Napoleon, possessing
the pounce of a true pagan,
would have been an after-
thought had he stopped at the

edge of his own known border.
History books would evaporate
if their subjects were not such
primordial hoarders. Perfection
anxiety has never occurred to

the coal miner or the foot soldier
or the concubine, or the polar
bear, for that matter, scrambling
through the rising glacier water,
searching for a broken berm of

ice to rest his skinny fur upon

THE NEUROLOGIST

after the orderly fourth
or fifth MRI and vague
generalities about pain
management we pass
the botox pump on
the way to surgical stasis
and there is a sense
of the body as a costly
bombed and plowed
battlefield and within
the splinters of silence
a lost eerie trumpet call
the tornado's aftermath
all through the gloom
snow leopards encroaching
on the hill but today
in the fractured light
thirty robins a cluster
of chickadees not
a murmuration but
an ostentatious cardinal
winds through the
proceedings probing
the dirt's black spine
consecutive turns
in their political system
worms pulled like
strings of pink rubber
taffy between the
forceps of their beaks

BABY BOOMERS

We're at the age where half our lives
are spent practicing the acquired ritual
of watching the older ones die

holding their cupped hands
as they slide awkwardly
from the angled hospital slabs

and pad toward the bathroom
their gowns bunched and caught
on their hip like a tilted kilt

The mechanical beds groan up
beneath the weight of the sky's ornaments
under the twisted wreckage of the day

moaning the way a cruise ship might
swallowed in one great suck
by the savage deep

and all the trapped eyes sinking together
are sweeping their lights along
the sleepy trellis of the reef

and the only beings that resist
cough into the surf their bitter reflux
doubting there was ever any need

for their existence and find that
they are dying in a language
they have never understood

as they reach their turning point
and fail to turn
Guilt is assigned

its missionary position
in the cupboard of our bodies
We stick our black beaks

into every crash and crevice
and are sickened by the golden lights
flaring out of these cracks

like camera flashes or silent fireworks
and lily pads of evidence float past
the sickle cells of shed snakeskins

Bridal veils of fractured jellyfish
stick to our battered boat
as its leaky motor bleeds out

and the gray mist descends
when we sputter and buck
through the sweaty oil of another night

Our lives' floating library is upended
and the fluttering pages scatter
like pumpkin seeds on the pulsing surface

Our skin hisses dry in the heat
and the shining lures of our gilded denial
baptized with keen efficiency

crack like crab traps against the cliff rocks
In the pick holes blasted by wind
one open window lands a hook

and you pull that vision like a sled
loaded with the lead biscuits
of your past and each one

broken loose lifts your longing
How is it that a single star
can suddenly break its vow

and slide across the entire sweep of sky
or the body aging bloom into a cloud
of blood like an egg

coddled too long in the pot
The shot women rinse their lingerie
and bandages in the sink

their feathery geometry burst
into a plague of ringing phones
as the shrill EKG stabs its alarms

into the doughy silence
A faint smell of impending snow
strings its peril on the windowsill

and loosed from the dull beep
of your closing heart you think
There's nothing better than to eat

something sweet by the sea
even in this winter or especially then
pistachio and sugar baklava

in a Styrofoam shell
thin layers of honey dough
and frothing salt waves fill the air

with warm flakes making
the boardwalk faces turn and follow
in your fragrant wake

GASLIGHT: INAUGURATION DAY

My Movado stopped at 12:02
as the Slovenian First Lady
waltzed with Lincoln's Bible

above the frothing camera
crews, her steely mien unmoving
in the stew of eyes. Empty

bleachers buttressed the slow
motion parade, and the fire
trucks stalled. Mediocrity

flooded the National Mall.
Inauguration Day, a young man,
arms outstretched, 100 stories

above the city, on the Westgate
Bridge, held aloft by swirling
blue police lights, determined

to suicide. The President
declares that he alone can
repair the American carnage.

Breakfast on the terrace,
my croissant writhed and
began its buttered dive off

the deck. 20,000 riot cops
                              practiced restraint as their
bloody fingers loosened

                              round the protestors' necks.
Underwater, I prepare myself
                              for every kind of violence,

aware that resistance is
                              doggerel, and my mongrel love
opens wide. Born sick,

                              susceptible to hellish jealousy,
the President turned his hair
                              into a lucky knot. Ceremonial

power does not stop, or hasten
                              the sizzle of falling rain, or
bend the wind away from

                              the banal porticoes. Twitter-
in-Chief, the Cheeto Caligula
                              is easy prey, praying for

sanctuary, that his lid should
                              not flip mid-sentence.
Beginnings foreshadow,

                              prophecies founder, non-
linear arguments web

                              around us. The language

we speak affects the way

                              we think. Even if the future
leads, a frozen gap in time

embroiders the fresh dialectic,

                              a fact-free epoch, where
the present is a sliver,

                              transitive, vindictive, in-
capable of yielding to

                              propriety. Awakened to

this disquieting scene,

                              on the edge of my property,
thirty-seven perched vultures

                              in a dead cypress tree. The
First Lady's coif does not

                              shiver in the shifting wind.

THE AGNOSTIC

Nature selects for survival, Man, for appearance.
Our behavior evolves according to our needs.
Science, at war with Religion, reveals our origin.

That man is a beast, at least that much is certain;
The battlefields of Nature have never given him ease.
Dung beetles working the carrion, maggots sprung

from their blue black ooze, brutish reproduction
and the survival of louts, intent on spreading their
own versions of honor, duty-bound to lance

the boil of imagination. The loss of faith is a slow
process, like the raising of continents from the eternal
rush of water, and the deposits engendered there,

layer upon layer, trembling with extinction.
What was once a free-swimming creature
finds itself glued by the head to a rock.

DICHOTOMIES

WORLD BOOGIE

Having just reached a rapport
        with piedmont flat South Carolina
before the John Calhoun Parkway
        smoothed out along the Savannah River
and the caveat of James Brown Boulevard
        wafted like a sweaty cape and intersected
with the Harriet Tubman Avenue alongside
        the Jefferson Davis Memorial Highway,
before I was sodden drunk on Partridge Inn
        bourbon and the expensive perfume of Augusta
Country Club socialites, Morphine was slowly
        droning on the stereo as I steered the old silver
Mercedes through Heritage Corridor between
        Johnston and Trenton where all the children go
to Strom Thurmond High School and the state
        income taxes are paid with peach profits,
ageless orchards cha cha in copious rows,
        dissecting the horizon, their low branches
nonchalantly slung at disinterested angles
        like cigarette girls resting their tired arms
against the wall, ignoring the casino's cacophony

PORTRAIT OF THE ARTIST AS A SPARK

Between the gas and the can
my lower leg disappeared
in a blue and orange flame.

Nothing is more articulate than fire.
It moves in slow motion
at the speed of light,

a ragged language, raw and messy,
that leaves a shattered
chugging trail of shadows and debris,

the charred coals of a formerly
living thing. Fire never mutters.
it barks with surprise,

then shrieks, tears apart the precision
of speech, and leaves a soiled scar
of broken sentences.

Impaled on a spit,
clarity returns in a burst.
Thirty-five years ago, what

hung a flaming necktie round
my tender brain, and begged through
the spindle of my body

for some sudden flash of truth?
Fire filled my veins.
Poetry pulled me out by the roots.

TRANQUILITY & TREMOLO

Where song is, fire begins, tightens,
then leaps to scream with such ease
that every awkward thing is quickly consumed.

We are upended by the creaks and turns of language,
and the truth is not uplifting, though the mod historians
idolize the facts just enough to reduce their significance.

You can't find the right style to defeat vulgarity;
or stage manage a grizzly bear. Besides, says the famous
novelist, evil has its own reveille, and I never compart-

mentalize, because you rent the fabric of the narrative
that way and all these boxes of chaos, contained in
closets, cosseted by doors and boards, does not

allow the connective tissue to nest its webbing
in your life. But poets are fractured and unfulfilled,
walking on the fragments of language like a child

measuring the steps upon rocks across a river.
The camera lens is capable of great destruction,
and that recognition is what caused you to leave

your body from the first charge of a fragrance,
that smell and memory are connected in the brain,
your mother's brownies, a new car, a nearby skunk,

fresh cut lawn, a rotting corpse, and every lover who
attracted you, with their invisible chemicals filling
your senses, and when that smell glitters, the entire body

is fluorescent and wedded to that glowing instance.
The cripple is interested in shoes and smells leather
everywhere. A burning tire rolls past in a black night

and bounces against an unseen wall. Flames fly off
like orchid petals. Buttoned tight, the words strain
against their cuffs like beads on a shaken abacus,

moving without purpose on an iron track,
until a train appears and all the meaning stands,
emerging from the smoke of garbled intentions,

its one bright lamp slicing through the polluted
darkness and the poem is that beam, long perfected
and lethal, like a slinky the size of a boa made of steel.

THINKING, FAST AND SLOW

We are blind
about our own blindness
and exaggerate
our opinions and impressions
couch our judgements
in hyperbole and forget
how utterly unknowable
the world is
The careful myth
of objectivity peels
when the car brakes suddenly
and the deliberate feeling
of the mind like a glacier
slowly moving over
vast reserves of information
is jerked into paying
insurance money to terrorists
in Thailand
the domain of dice-throwing
monkeys who train fighter pilots
to love the blue flame
of their brains
and forget their expertise
among like-minded lovers
of rational procrastination
analyzing happiness
in increments
of chrysanthemums
Sometimes a great notion
gets rescued from the slush pile
and we are saved

THE SOUL IN MARBLE

From the age of eight, sketching Paul's likeness
for the Pope and touted as the greatest sculptor
since Michelangelo, Bernini set about proving
this premonition, milking from marble the fire

that first created the Earth itself, finding his spark
through St. Lawrence's horrid barbecue, the floral
odor of roasting flesh. Then the artist's rage uncovered
Costanza, humped by his brother, and he tried to murder

his sodomizing sibling beneath the canopy of St. Paul's
Cathedral, and as a coup de grâce, hired an assassin to slash
poor Costanza's perfect cheeks. Those rough scars were
mounted at the base of the Basilica, veins that spread

across the facade, creeping from the weakness,
cracking the foundations of faith, as Bernini's bell
tower was demolished, one cut brick at a time.
Bernini diminished the nymph, Daphne, released her

to the gods in her first moment of womanhood,
as she turned into a sturdy laurel tree, protected for all
eternity from the clutches of men, then her shoulders
separated and the branches leapt, the reach of her

agony stretching out her raised fingertips into shimmering
leaves and for miles around all the locals looked up,
covered in the raining flakes and startled by her screams.
And so, Bernini the prodigy became the laughingstock

of Rome, planning the colonnades of his miraculous
return, the confidante of Popes who splashed his hope
in the everlasting Spanish parable starring St. Teresa
of Avila, levitating and penetrated by angels with golden

arrows, over and over, as she moaned, craving the horn.

TENDING THE PLOW

Watched my parents having sex,
eight or nine I was,
quiet as a cotton wad, stuck my
one eye in the door
crack, and wondered about the
jerking and the jiggling
flesh on their backs. Diddled my
high school girlfriend
in the music room, and watched
the fiddle's strings
tighten and constrict, her frightened
hips quivering as
the melody dripped out. My wife's
friend can't send
nude pictures of herself to her
incarcerated husband,
though I watched a Kardashian
flash the entire
world, looping a perfect arc of
fizzing champagne,
its release timed to land in a glass
perched precariously
on the shelf of her robust naked ass.
Her well-oiled breasts
and back were provided in separate
blooming shots,
though it is OK, says the warden,
for the wife to send
pictures of her lovely feet. So far
as I can see, the plow

stays sharp in the field. No matter
how long the rows,
the urge to merge with another grows
more poignant toward
dark, all eyes on the parallel horizon.
So long as you
tend to the sweet singing, let the scythe
blade ring, and
massage all the stubborn edges into a
fine whistling line.

JENNY STARLING'S CLASSIFIED INFORMATION

The secretary's main ambition, raising protocol,
And dull to the flaming day,
She composes a note, classified information:

Lonely Super Hero seeks Lovely Same.
He appeared, optimum guile, bearing pie.
Summoned by her poetry, pledged devotion.

Quickie marriage, off the beaten path;
El Paso, anal sex, blazing saddles.
Puppy love's destruction, greet the priest

Annul the potato, meet the parents.
Intermittent miracles amid disappointment, this life.
It all depends on the contrary;

Opposite sex, we'd rather not know.
Shuffled decks, our heroine defies memory,
And with newfound vigor, returns hunting.

Fantastic Animal, Fifty and Still Snarling,
The hook line blared, classified victorious.
If summoned, give your life poetry.

WONDER WOMAN

Only a man who has lived
with his wife and mistress
under the same roof
would invent the polygraph.
The kind of worker bee
who figured out how
to strike a match and set
the entire hive on fire.

Who would build a heroine
as sexy as Gypsy Rose Lee,
whose assets would never sag,
then wrap her in an American flag,
her tiara a nice touch,
invoking a royal status
and keeping her wild mane
in check at the same time,

as bullets bounced off her bracelets
and hardened criminals crumpled
in confusion when wrapped
in her golden lariat of truth.
Justice was no big commodity
in 1941 on Paradise Island
where everyone was super
and no one need trumpet
their austerity or power.

Wonder Woman flew
her invisible plane
and claimed
the constant repercussions
of man's deception lie
in his rampant materialism
and everything valuable
that I know I have learned
from two beautiful women
said William Moulton Marston.

A GIRL LIKE THAT

Being talented means you are
acutely aware of your limitations,
and that becomes unbearable.

What was once so available
has now become a terrible note,
and the intuition, a shining knife.

The whole hidden world is in love
with virility, forgetting the sick fertility
of a trellised animal mind.

The perfect actress never asks why
the flowers sit up high in their buckets,
lit from behind by tiny strobes of light.

A girl like that can make
a man go mad with pleasure,
one who strips the taboos away.

Simone de Beauvoir would say
I was betrayed by the rain,
thinking my persona could withstand

any eraser, and Time laughs
banging the dust off his shoes
on the wall, his calf caught with

a twinge of pain inside his pants.
On his knees the tile floor taught
him what the booze could not,

a woman like that makes your
extremities numb, the long years
of blues slogans are wrung

repeatedly from your descriptions
of her friends. The waiting never ends
and the dull night's loose ends

are lit by the tight fuse of her smile
and she licks her lips
as your straw is repeatedly stabbed

into the ice, her eyes' begging lashes
batting twice as you take the stand,
plastic comb teeth broken between

your hands, lost trail of sentences
wandering into the blue distance.
The red windows in her room are

wrapped round the sun's gold marble,
a fleck of it startling the prison birds
as they turn and follow her out

into the yard, so vivid, yellow
and green, grass not quite high
enough to hide the scars.

LOVE AMONG CANNIBALS

In the wilderness of mirrors,
carving History from black stone,
he was built with books
and regular in his habits.
The experiments tested his limits;
and though he sometimes preferred
the sizzle to the steak, his reputation
was made by swallowing shadows.
All black dishes are expensive,
olives, peppered crab cake, currant,
caviar, vanity buttressed by the
powder of a rhino's horn,
or black truffles poised in cream,
or diabolical shark fin soup.
Romance makes History bearable,
gives it sauce, even the sadists
propped on top of the anniversaries
of their actions, like grooms
on wedding cakes, are lost
in their appetite's labyrinth.
The Elizabethans were appalled
upon their discovery of cannibalistic
tribes, but were cooked and
consumed just the same.
The woman who wishes to possess
her lover would never think
of eating him, though her metabolism
would certainly squire some
of his cells into secret hiding places,
pieces squirreled away in case

of calamity, like all things we ingest,
processed for nutrition or waste,
or some bits which are especially
prized for their toxicity,
that the rusting body politic must
zealously protect, fueling the cocktails
for the ferryman, who sharpens
his teeth on a buffet of bones,
and steers his dark boat between
the meal's breaking crusts.

ROBERT JOHNSON'S
MILK COW BLUES

We love the singer for the ache in his voice.
We love the acre for the seam of water
splitting it in two. Neither of them know
the source of the bruise, or why the blunt blue
cut that pushes back against their best efforts
so transfixes the visitors, who cannot avert
their own pitiless gazes or suppress their
best guesses about the fault's black back history.
The brindle cow grazes and chews and stares into
the indigo pool that divides the field, a song in
her head that calls across the fracture toward her calf,
hobbling like a toddler in its mother's leathery heels,
its rubbery wheels drunkenly reeling the calf toward
its only recognizable song, regardless of the source.

LOUIS AND THE WOLF

I have come to wonder if Louis Armstrong
and The Wolf ever met—what a sight that,
a grand summit meeting complete with growling,
Wolf licking his harp and Satchmo grinning away,
deftly fingering his horn in an effort to curtail
the sonic boom of the two most powerful voices
ever gathered in the walls of a single room.
Snarling and stalking that elegant whisper,
I imagine Wolf laying tracks and Louis so
remarkably dignified, so clearly in the furrows
of the groove, prowling the stage like the shadow
of a storm cloud while Wolf raged and bit down
on the low chord changes like a chainsaw blade,
a ragged sound refined by the shimmering honey
of the Great Dipper's rising horn, so perfectly
above the fray. Howling down on all fours,
writhing on the stage and King Louis, with his
handkerchief flying like a flag on a mahogany
galleon, hurtling across the choppy sea's wake.
Wolf, bursting with Delta moan and the evil
ways of a tail dragger for Satan, forsaking his
mother's gospel hysterics and earning her
undying neglect, right up to his final deathbed.
Named for a president, Chester Arthur Burnett
was born under a bad sign, Haley's Comet
burning across the sky like a brakeman's lantern,
but a bluesman will survive, staring straight into
the sun like a rifle with eyes. Old Satch would
know, his thunderous percussive purr emerging
from the earth like a fountain of pent-up feeling,

meticulous in its placement as it repeatedly
echoed the punch of the brass lines and the
cymbal set to ride. His cornet weathered
every swinging era, Bird's heebie jeebies
and the Big Band's muskrat rambles, always
sailing and seldom misbehaving, not since
the rancid Storyville days and the Colored
Waif's Municipal Boy's Home, his body
peppered black and blue with blows until
the bent boy escaped via the Mississippi on
a light-littered steamboat, its giant wheel
just the juju and propulsion needed to heal
the nuance of a genius whose rules are its own,
and those last quiet notes with the crowd so still
you could hear a rat pissing on cotton, the gleaming
corner of a note set to crackle, piercing the racial
gloom of the American heart like buckshot,
his trumpet bell uplifted and ringing. And though
the rain may ooze and lovers lose that feeling,
the moon melt down and the earth finally find
its ceiling in the poisoned heavens, there will
still be a sound overwhelming all others, a horn
poised flaming in our imagination, though the
earth be smothered and fire rise a final time
inside the webbing of our skin. *One touch of
nature makes the whole world kin*, said Ulysses
to a pouting Achilles, his own mind boiling
with the shock of recognition, both bound
in worship like Louis and the Wolf, whose
dream meeting probably never took place,

though my mind cannot erase the wish of it,
the sheer bliss and pitch and rich opposition
that the scene presents, a listening like I have
never experienced, gears within gears grinding
until the wounds are wound together, the grace
of music calming every child's feathers, arm in arm
as they rise and sing in the Gulf's fearsome swelter.

THIS ROCK IS GONNA ROLL

The Bobby Soxers that swooned at The Copa
turned absolutely feral at the sight of Elvis

whose pelvis punched vibrant holes
in the flaming statutes of the US Senate

Subcommittee on Juvenile Delinquency.
Alan Freed blew their little minds on his

front lawn in Newark, *rock and roll* dancing
is the only way to go, Daddio, he asserts,

and Muddy Waters followed the guiding
star to a stable in Memphis, country and blues

had a baby, he said, and they named it
rock and roll. Big Mama Thornton's

country hound clowned around and bit
Sam Phillips whose giant Sun Studios

puts the entire nation in shadow. Never mind
that, Bill Haley's Comet careened from the dark

and *Rocked* Around the Clock, his jet fuel just
juicy enough to let Big Joe Turner Shake, Rattle

and *Roll*. The planet recovered its bearings
and ironed its wobble long enough to regain

the Red paranoia of the status quo. Come back,
said the King, there's Good *Rocking* Tonight

and he drove 'em mad in Jacksonville just
in time for Robert Zimmerman's bar mitzvah.

Roll With Me, Henry, Etta James caterwauled
and all this fine jockey and juke wax appalled

the good white folks who groused about these
kids and their abominable noises and aborigine

mating dances whose diseased hips made most
Alabamans concerned that this *rock and roll*

was a nefarious racial plot and giving their kids
poor diction and communicable treasonous lips,

but *rock* made a boat and *rolled* on the waves
to London where Studio 51 was soon to open

with Rory Blackwell's roaring *Rock 'N' Rollers*
and The Coney Island Kids formed their own

political third party campaigning for a growler,
a mandate which allowed for a *Rock & Roll*

President and the election was held at once.
Evidence to the contrary was immediately

thrown out of the court of public opinion.
Love Me Tender and Don't Be Cruel, grinned

the undisputed King, who took his tools
to Hollywood and ignored the Songs For

Swinging Lovers, the **Rock and Roll** Waltzes,
the schmaltz of top hat hound dogs and dying

Tommy Dorsey's gestalt of orchestral Cubism
and just took his assault to the kids who were

all shook up with these musical tales and
proved the hip adage that is true to this day,

just sneak up and grab a cool cat by the tail and
you will discover things you can learn no other way.

GLENN GOULD IN CARNEGIE HALL, 1962

Before the first note is struck,
the entire score is roused and swaddled
in the player's body.

Who is the Boss, when intimacy is broken,
and bow ties are straightened,
and any D minor concerto happens?

By 1964, Gould gave the Bernsteins
of the world a raspberry, and never
fingered the keyboard again
in a live setting.

When people leave their land
and heritage and head North,
what parts of themselves
are left behind?

Music is meant to be interpreted,
another language, available
to widows, and orphans,

and sea creatures,
who sing one to the other.
Inside a melody, we are never alone.

But the audience is a mob,
with variable perspectives,
an angle grinder lost to democracy,
and obsessed with Petula Clark.

From above, bridges are semi-colons
to the flow of the river's sentence,
and the beaches blaze,
holding the ocean in their frame.

From above, a baby grand
resembles the handle of a gun,
gold strokes slow the blood's roll,

and in this constraint,
the music is made,
and violently overflows.

"*LIKE A BUDDHA*, PAUL MOTIAN SAYS . . ."

When Paul Motian played drums
he seemed hardly there,
a swish, a stir, and then
with the whimsy of a ghost
slowly rising from the vent,
several frozen colors came
splashing rapidly down
like flushed birds in the distance.
It's the sound an exploding dandelion
might make, if it were made of tin,
when all else stopped
and silence strained at its bit,
listening for him.

I support the band, he asserted.
I am an accompanist.
There to make it happen, not to linger,
like when I made Monk twirl,
he says, stirring the air with his finger.
What else is there? He shrugs,
plays with his teeth. I know that
a far greater country exists, he asserts.
I have set my foot down on it,
many rhythms occurring all at once,
layers of strings. His eyebrows sting
and sharpen, why ask? He is restful
and folds his hands inside one another.

There are perfectly good explanations
for the simultaneous risks we juggle.
There are shipyards of baubles
and harbors that have dried up
and martinis made up by Episcopalians
that burnish them for the plagiarisms
of the Holy Spirit. It's only right
that the room is furnished
with importance and low light.
Gotta flaunt the groove, with flourishes
and gentle force, I guess.
Like a Buddha, Paul Motian says.

THE KICK OF INFINITY: PARADOXICAL ARCHITECTURE

for Christopher Nolan and Kurt Cobain

Our dream of rock and roll
the unholy madness of feigned apathy
is so much greater than its reality

Folding the landscape requires
tapping the unfulfilled potential
of the infectious imagination

and seeing the museum
the attendant park and fountain
the regular motion of the automobiles

lay over at right angles
to the horizon
like a giant lawn chair

and provide a ceiling
to the cafe talk and ritual
destruction of the buttered croissants

Our dream feels the vivid moment
when the mind and the body
have been most married

when the power of the body's
rhythmic forces are marshaled
in the service of a dancing mind

a joy so complete that all the world
is saved from its own horrid limbo
of tribal fear and inadequacy

bolted in a blinking roller coaster
that is endlessly falling
like an accordion constellation from the sky

The paramount narrative exists
in a parallel dimension sifting
among emotional sea surges

just as a poem must begin
in the thicket of the mind's
predicament without benefit

of a sensible back story
how you might have arrived
in the thick of action

gone so horribly wrong
freight trains slowly
ascending off their tracks

rooftop shingles letting go
trees uprooted and flying
upside down into space

the rote cycles of the road
answering only to the puzzles
of appetite and popular earworms

the coaster rolling so solid
on its convenient wheels
moments before and then

like a charm bracelet sprawling
broken from its wrist suddenly seeing
in the weightless instant the seat

empty beside you as your
realization explodes with your heart
into the frozen carnival ground

THE INVISIBLE BRIDGE

Inside the Space Station, amnesia's simple fog
is added to the litany of our growing physical
concerns. What are we without our memories?

Each meaningful success is littered with false starts,
lost in the gray mist as the great sun comes, and we
are stumbling about in our bulky suits, lunging

at every flicker of affection, caught in the gears
of the imagination's great harem, washed clean
of an earthbound past and its requisite boundaries.

Oblivious to recent mistakes, and insatiably curious,
the steaming brain rides on its spiral post like a train
gliding from station to station, gathering loaded

cars for its final climb. Behind us, the weight
of dreams slows our roll. Remember everything
and you have the record of each fugitive slight,

losing the ability to forgive. In the constant
process of regeneration, the logbooks fill up
with observations, and every 92 minutes,

another poem comes shining. We let our arms
drift out in the free gravity, and float past one
another silently, becoming the revolution

that is urged forward. Gathering clouds of carbon
migraine through the brittle space around us.
Since every second of our existence is expensive,

our peers are shot with excitement during each
mistake, filled with the terror of a loosened bolt.
We keep our shattered parts tucked out of sight.

We are filled with a beauty we cannot reflect,
and as we move from chamber to chamber,
we fly straight through without touching

the sides. Sometimes we drive with our knees,
and our big toes are calloused from pushing off.
Our eyesight is constantly getting worse,

so we listen with our whole beings, and forget
where we put the remote, the bandages, the keys.
We are moving ten times the speed of a bullet

and have no control. In the darkness we have
become the thing that the others fear most.
Unable to sleep and numb inside our own country,

we are lost in translation and free from familiars.
Invisible specters, holding between their hands
our most precious deconstructions, carve our

reflections into time's rough passage. Playing from behind the practiced persona of lightly smoked glass, we fling paper airplanes; we do lonely things.

THE HIDDEN LIFE OF ANTS

How many times in the last twenty-five years
has my beautiful wife stabbed a needle into
the same pin cushion and withdrawn it,
leaving no discernible mark? A point made
by Baudelaire of Satan, noting that his greatest
trick was to convince so many that he didn't
even exist. Still the tomato-sized pillow takes
its constant pricking and hides the holes,
filled to the gills with doll-sized Excaliburs
jammed willy-nilly into its epidermis, a crown
of swords it proudly displays, and with great
intestinal fortitude, it dissuades the scarred
remnants of the puncture's aftermath.

With no memory, the Mud God digs through
the depleted Thames and its retracted tides
for historical artifacts to connect himself to the past.
Whatever one makes of the young blades and
their chiliastic death cults, constantly recalibrating
the date of the apocalypse, like a nest of blinded
Cyclops feeling around the cave wall for relief
or news of Armaggedon, a portion of their calvary
is aiding the Mud God as he rubs a rose farthing
between his thumb and forefinger and tosses it into
the bin with the ferry tokens, clay pipes, and Tudor
hairpins, portions of memory dislocated by mini
tremors of history when the light was out and aesthetic
outbursts left no discernible mark in the moist muck.

All the ants are wandering single file through
the nail holes of a horseshoe, left beside the
pewter badge of its master, a pilgrim mount
returning from Canterbury Cathedral, on the
foreshore between Westminster and Wapping,
the north river docking Roman, Saxon, Viking
and Norman conquerors, who are all now just
pins on a map. The centuries-old legs of the rickety
pier surround the larks rolling in mud, scattering
the ants on what was once the flood plain of
a mighty and venerable cushion that carried
centuries of ships softly through the bristling city,
unfurling their ribbons upon a river named Thames.

GAZA

Fifty-two circles round the Sun,
the defeated armies shut down
and head home, mannequins

of porcelain dancing past
their splinters, making mentors
of their monsters, and the architecture,

listening, buttered by the culture,
reflects the fissures in the structure.
Pearl-covered prophets, tenderized

by indifference, are heralded
as sorcerers, their cults of flying
monkeys forming the basis

for the new psychiatry. Surveillance
and suspicion are twins, guided
by the genius of Paradise.

The stories fill a golden chalice,
and the makers are the mission's
memory, stalks of corn remaining

from the crop circles and theories
of alien creation. Judaculla Rock
and the rumors of the dead, travel up

and down escalators in our heads.
The rain on the roof, like little fists,
is harmless it seems, 'til like

an unraveling mountain, the smallest
stones fall with great force
and increasing collaboration

on the placid village beneath,
like a blister on a bee that undoes
the colony. Urizen is an after-throb

in this ectoplasmic blur, and emerges
from the Nile like a soggy cur
of the absolute. A curtain of loose hair

flies round his head like a halo.
Blake & John Clare samba gently past
the body on the smashed bleeding moor.

FRAGMENTS OF A DOOR

for Gorky, Flanagan, Maurer,
Pascin, Modigliani, and Lehmbruck

Gray is a stabilizing serum
when the vocabulary of the circle
stands in opposition to the world.
Bodies collide and Art is the result,
fragments of a door from houses built
to be exploded, where each capricious
form seeks accompaniment,
and pain is rarely pastel.

Then the mothering layers of paint
are applied, as the model holds
her breath, and the decades are laid
in strips, cambium layers coursing
and then the common corrosion,
starring the body as a rusted cage,
bulging with minerals returning
to their original state.

In this disturbia, Disraelis of disreality,
vampires copulating with dying sharks
aboard venal yachts, and slaughterhouses
of curved cattle offering their backs
to the blade. The dog, that is rendered motionless
by the sound of its master's voice, hears cruelty
in the cock's herald, and dreads the executioner
slowly combing his hair.

Seated before Nature, who rents the things
she loves, what is reflected is elsewhere,
in what may come, in cumbersome numbers,
long dripping entrails hanging from the trees,
or pardoned and buoyantly loved, the protected
titans of business sidle like rabbits into their warm
cubbyholes, and behold upon their walls
the portals of infinity they have purchased.

STYLISH VIOLENCE

The essential American soul
is hard, isolate, stoic and a killer.
It has never yet melted. —D. H. Lawrence

Into this life I'm poured,
a trip wire, and the tears
I shed yesterday, whose
circumference are everywhere,
have become rain.

I am your horrible fate
because you called for it.
The writer is a cruel god,
who imitates his Father
as best he can, who longs

to make something of lasting beauty,
dire and slanted, facing in all
directions, separate elements
stabbing like bayonets into the vortex
of their stylish intentions,

a radiant node or cluster of ideas
that concentrate the mind
wonderfully and in its wake
the violence freezes memorable
mythologies in their place.

And the monument, or country,
or studio, never stands free of its
guide wires, its story trundled
like a spider logrolling its fly,
or Rapunzel tangled and hung

in the glorious chords of hair,
unaware that the action has curdled,
tentacles of gunfire reach past,
and gunned quick engines,
crunching metal, are slickly

blistered in shrink-wrapped
mementos flashing past our numbed
sight lines without chilling effect.
Silently, the result cuts ditches
in our national conscience,

and centuries of good will
drain away. Glitches and tape
delays keep the stars stitched
to their schedule. The magic
bullets miss the villain and he rises.

I live with a witch, a real one,
whose mystery is her talisman,
whose many faces overlap,
whose history parallels the paradigm
of this world and its newly

darkened ages. Who walks the beach
edge and moans and paces and claps.
I am ridden, and do her bidding
willingly. The nefarious ostentatiousness
of this time reveals the vanity

of the silkworm in its quest to bloom.
No one is immune to the drive-by,
the random spree, the knock at the door,
and the stranger, straddling the original
choice, with a whirlwind for a voice.

THE SEARCHERS

Sometimes you move through weathered
monuments and find a place to set your lens
for all time, or like Ford's withered
protagonists, you gain your prize at
the cost of all else. Or like the wounded
McCandless and Treadwell, with no star
to fix their flight, who found an Alaska
to eat or be eaten by, whose magical carpet
ride unraveled at the feet of their Maker,
with no exotic Marrakesh springing to sing
them perfumed songs of last-minute escapes.

Ansel Adams likened color photography
to playing an out of tune piano, conflicted
by the adventure of developing it, but his
garish fantasies defined a dream of the
American West solidly lodged in the cortex
of fellow travelers in Grand Central Station,
his infinite scale making freedom a stern
train ride away. Wheeling through the flash
bulbs of the Cosmos, Einstein searched
the heavens to find some glimpse of God
staring back, some rhythm to jump start

his heart, yet as a musician, Einstein's
timing could best be described as extra-
dimensional, or had he been a drummer,
two shoes in a dryer, with minor misplaced
sonic booms disrupting the distant tapestry.
Every hero becomes a bore at last,
said Emerson, and discovery inconsequential.
Even Napoleon, on St. Helena, was obsessed
with the superiority of stout women, as he
picked through his breakfast of poached
eggs, asking "Can't I leave the battlefield,
even for a minute?"

Some poor souls seeking glory are left
wounded in their punitive wars and shot by
puny villagers for the gold in their teeth,
or some like Matthew Henson, drag their
black carcass and the frozen assets of
various companions to the top of the world,
only to be ignored by History. To be Gorky
is to discover pools of radiant color clawing
through your canvas, or soap bubbles
bouncing in airborne arcs like children
on rainbow swings delivering abstract
masterpieces from the bowels of Armenian

massacres and to hold your mother,
dying from hunger, in your arms.
To mesmerize others, one must see the worst
of the world's colors, to lift your saber like
General Lee in the direction of eternity,
to find your final resting place being whipped
through gauntlets of defeat and disgrace,
to clamber over the unassailable precipice
and drop into nothing at your life's expense,
to fight out from the bottom or through the wall,
and discover that the journey itself was its own
reward, and that the ardent search was all.

CARAVAGGIO'S CARNAL GOSPEL

Jailed for a dollop of poetry, a fugitive artichoke,
a scabbard filled with an oily sword, a swollen
corpse housing the Holy Mother, whose ascent,
(or lack of it) horrified the Carmelite sisters.

Life for Caravaggio was a duel to the Death
with tradition itself, his head on a pike
like John the Baptist, wanted dead or alive
by friend and foe alike. Terrified, erotic and hysterical,

Carravagio's card players called to a corrupt Bacchus,
sacred grapes gripped in squalid fingers, glimmering
in the darkness, a music that seduces even St. Matthew
in the midst of martyrdom, cherubs whose iris eyes

reflect the shattered glass of the plague, dogs walking
upright through the back alley, sticking their paws
into the open wound of Jesus, a carnal Gospel,
whose weight pinned Paul like a centipede.

BROKEN INTO LIGHT

Nothing in the universe is stationary.
Everything is in motion, the foundation
under your house, the giant rock in the

pasture where you played Cowboys and
Indians as a child, the tree that made
the oranges for your breakfast juice.

And though the face would seem to
possess an endless array of shapes,
it can only make 21 expressions or

recognizable emotions, and to lose
face is to have your pride ripped
away, and the light in your eyes

will have suddenly changed, moving
as it is toward all the nothing rushing
silently past your perception, which

only sees 1% of the electromagnetic
spectrum and hears less than 1% of
the acoustic buffet of sounds, even

the atoms in your body are made up
of 99.9% empty space, and none of
those are the ones you were born with.

You have two less chromosomes than
a common potato, and the existence of
that rainbow in the distance depends

upon the conical photoreceptors in your
eyes, because the animals without these
cones cannot see it, meaning that you

don't just look at the rainbow, you also
create it. How many of the highways
in the mind do we ever traverse? And

what junk does the suffocated spirit
find necessary as we hurtle across the
galaxy at 220 kilometers per second?

Atoms and planets and blizzards and
bees, the trillions of black holes sucking
water down the toilet, the praying mantis

that bites off the head of her suitor, does
she see, in her limited lonely view, a galaxy
of possibilities, as she looks down the blank

neck of her dead mate, with her five compound
eyes, like staring at the blue haze of a movie
screen without the benefit of 3-D glasses?

The Mexican cavefish and the hammerhead
shark both feel the lateral lines and electric
pulses of the very land itself as they glide

congruently through the dark water, a grid
in their minds pulling them forward. Some
folks believe they should let their light shine

bright, let their perfect voice sing and fill
the world, but it is clear that most people's
light is much more dim than they think;

and it might be better if that brimming glow
were internalized, blowing open their fragile
bodies, like a chandelier with lances of pure

light poking out in every direction, a porcupine
of moonlit sabers, looking just as pitiful, in
stark relief, as that fat, humpbacked, waddling

little Yoda of quills and shivers, a dire,
fearful pincushion, ready to stab you in
as many places as it can and run away.

Van Gogh's depictions of natural phenomena
are near perfect renderings of turbulence,
one of the last unsolved mysteries of classical

physics, his *Starry Night, Road with Cypress
and Star, Wheatfield with Crows* were all
painted during periods of prolonged psychosis,

either chained in an insane asylum, or created
just before his suicide, when he was warped
by hallucinations. Even bees, raised in a lab,

prefer Vincent's *Sunflowers* to the real thing.
In a dark time, the eye begins to see, sd. Ted
Roethke, no stranger to mental illness himself.

The fundamental tool of astronomy is still
the eye, aided by telescopes and cameras,
as the light in our bodies, moving through

the trees of lymphatic vessels, and the brain's
veins and secretions, sees its mirror roiling
and exploding across an atmosphere we

barely know, expanding faster than we can
understand. Before this poem is over, your
body will have produced a million billion

new antibody molecules, more stars than
grains of sand on a beach will have blown
apart, and their light will not reach us for

thousands of years, though they, and we,
will be long cold, the ganglion cells of our
retinas no longer firing back at the heavens

with any reflected glory, the seasons lost,
the reasons muddled, the body's breakage
just the basis for another forgotten poem.

BLUE MOUNTAIN PANORAMA

I craned my head and listened hard,
                    the blues were speaking,
2500 feet up Mount Ararat,
                    riding the Lincoln Highway,
where the homespun Allegheny
                    Mountains meet the nonlinear
patchwork knobs of the spent
                    Pennsylvania Appalachia.
German Dutch and Amish squares
                    are interrupted by the chess pieces
of church spires, silent giant windmills
                    spread across the bald ridges,
like trees without their gown of leaves,
                    spinning their mantis arms to catch
the flow that fuels the towns. I remembered
                    dragging planks up to the thick
midsection of the old Fraser pine
                    and built a five-story landing
that allowed me to watch the world
                    unroll down the valley, and piling
hardened cow dung clods for games
                    of war in the rotting barn.
Barbed wire caught my sister once,
                    biting her wrist to the bone,
and I knew *the blues had spoken.*
                    The dirt roads were sprayed
with oil to keep the dust down,
                    the naked gourds were broken
during pumpkin season, and a juvenile
                    coon riveted a softball size

ornament on his snout, so eager
                        was he to get at the sweet meat.
So much peace it seems, but since
                        the Sun went dim, nothing keeps
the gold plague from approaching,
                        and *the blues have spoken.*
The deer population has exploded
                        and the resulting collisions
with motorists have strewn corpses
                        all along the road's shoulders.
Lazy buzzards ride the wind thermals
                        and circle like fixed gray drones.
Inside Tuscarora Mountain, the tunnels
                        are sheer behind the neighboring
cliffs and its inhabitants conduct
                        their unseen commerce, coiled tight
as a nautilus, and their hidden industry
                        enables the rise of the chattering
countryside. Their children get the honey
                        and the rest have grown pallid,
with violet lips, and they gather
                        together by the river to hear the governor
give the news. *The blues have spoken,*
                        he tells them, and in Newville,
where the heart of the Cumberland
                        Valley has begun to fray, the police
produce improved tasers and practice
                        on targets that bear our likeness,

and in this spreading world the mountain
                    removal has begun, just a little off the top
say the banker's sons, and distant wisps
                    grow into solid, smoldering columns
of mellifluous destruction, where the last
                    languid strains of smoke have broken
loose, and *the blues have spoken*.

NECROLOGIES

"SNOW IS GHOSTLY . . ."

Snow is ghostly.
Loosed by the certainty of its dominion
over the living,
as its baby traps fall in sheer numbers,
a brilliant
silence ensues, and the burrow of its cover
thickens and
glistens, as all stop purely to worship
its great weight
and myriad strategies for halting
the traffic,
upending the banker and beggar
alike, bending
the haughty oak and snapping its
branches, tacking
the planes to the ground. Happy
on its throne,
the white brows unfurrow and the
hair comes down.
A cold wind holds us fast in the
bright collision.

WHEN YOU GO TO GROUND

in memory of The Genie

It's the oddball you got to watch.
    A platypus is evidence that God
smokes pot, said Robin Williams,
    that poor supersonic clown, but
a duck-billed platypus is armed
    with venomous spurs on its
paddling back flippers, and will
    sink them into its enemy's deepest
epidermis and leave a hollowed
    carbuncle full of boiling poison.
Its aftermath makes a mamba bite
    look like a bee sting, and then the
clown, that is you, says, with the
    belt tightening around your neck,
I went for this serene evening dip,
    and all seemed calm, until I got
killed by a platypus pitching southpaw,
    and there he goes, swimming
sweetly off to join his ersatz family,
    those zany evolutionary mistakes,
chirping in code, and splitting up the
    long night's ration of crawdads,
gathered round the tiny dining table,
    safely away from human pesticides,
spry crocodile snouts, and unseen hawk
    talons, tucked all together in some
warm dark welcoming hole called home.

THOUGHTS ON EASTER
WHILE DIGGING A GRAVE

Once there were so many buffalo rumbling
on the Great Plains, they darkened the landscape
like a storm, so many that trains full of men,
armed with carbines, would fly through the West
shooting the animals dead, stopping only long
enough to load up the skins, boxcar after boxcar
of bloody fun, leaving behind pyramids of skulls
at every station.

Fully loaded, lovely, oblivious
and muscular, three neighbor boys, with skull
plates thin as a dime, and the Southern sun settled
hissing in the bog behind their eyes, have tacked
sixteen new raccoon skins to their leaning barn
wall this Spring. At 4:00 am, with cats afuzz in the
walls, they tree a young coon one hundred feet
from our bedroom window, and shake him out
to the dogs.

With shards of the sun still plaguing
my sleepy eyes, I see in first light that the dogs
have done their best and still the animal offered
to them is moving inside his radiant skin. Too
stunned to focus down the geometry of my rifle's
sight, I miss everything and then gather my wits
to commit to the deed and slowly squeeze the
easy trigger.

Pontius, prone to murder, was not
comfortable as a killer in the public eye, washed
his hands of all complicity in an act of political
theater, but still stacked another skull on the pile
that formed the mound at Golgotha, and gave the
mob the blood they needed to sate the pain from
the various splinters that had compromised their
fractured lives.
            I cannot say if the dove of peace
flew from His cave on that third day. I was not
there to verify the scars or countenance the final
resting place of the torn robes that contained His
light. Evidence of things unseen make His passing
no less a crime, or lessen His deeds, marked on these
simple blooming dogwood trees that are maturing
much too soon.
            I am only left with a shovel and no
soft peace in the forest's closing room. I break the
ground and lay him down as the flies work to suture
his wounds. We are given these deeds and without
hate or grief, thread our choices, to ease some suffering
and do no harm, in the shadow of a crumbling barn.
I lean on this handle and ponder a heaven for animals,
some dark rustling

renowned for its guardians, a golden
stream filled with succor and dreams; of crawdads that
swim into your paws, to walk unmolested in the light
of day and never hide your flaws, or fear the same rude
tenor, defeated by the claws of constantly greater mentors.
The art of survival is a story that ends too soon, a lesson
learned this morning, after the unceremonious shooting
of a single innocent coon.

THE LONG BLACK ROAD

Having been chased into the roar and clash,
trapped on the Pennsylvania Turnpike,

even the ten-point buck, agile as he was,
could not escape; no way to fudge this.

The first car caught him square on the
right back flank and cast him airborne.

Through some miraculous twist, or will,
he managed to land on his feet, only to

discover that the back half didn't work,
and he used his front hooves to scramble

and claw to the fence, where he wedged
his head and jerked beneath it as best he could,

his only thought the darkness of the woods.
There he flopped and writhed, still firmly

in this world, his frantic mind wracked with pain.
Ink blot clouds were nosing across the sunny

mountainside, like the shadows of giant fish
moving just beneath the surface of the sea.

The trooper on the scene would not discharge
his weapon, too much paperwork for that, so I

finally did it, finished the buck with a baseball bat.
It was all I had, and washed the bashed brains

off the wood of my Louisville Slugger with water
I had saved to drink. Sometimes I think what

it must be like for an animal to encounter a road.
Same as a human watching figures in flight,

bouncing across the surface of the moon,
some vacant place without oxygen or light,

one wrong move from death's certain broom.
Damn things ought to learn, the trooper said,

and turned his back on the night. All the drivers
steered past, thankfully trapped behind their steel

and glass, their futures fixed and their suitcase
packed, right foot planted firmly on the gas.

SHADES OF NIGHT DESCENDING

in memory of N. Mailer

Coming upon his death today, the radio
pulling my car along, and beside us
in undulating waves, the wind rocks
the spikes of wheat, stalks of light
mocking the indigent roads, a golden
surf of espaliers and whippets whispering
excitedly alongside the harsh laws of
the highway and its gravity, sculpting
the mountain's stout neck with veins
of access, lining the landscape's face
with violet wrinkles, interrupted only
by Norman's familiar voice and sprinkles
on the windshield, silver bells of rain.

These desolate miracles occur every day,
in the shades of night descending, and
the moon atop the mountain, lying
on its back, entitled to verticality,
is languid and sordid at once, coarse
as Norman was, with the space
collapsed around the moon face and
all weight drawing the hills to express
their full height and majesty in response.
The revolutions of Nature are silently
at work, a chromatic, diabolical fugue
is laid upon the night's baton.
Traduced by these memories, alone
this moment in America, I see the moon,
emptied, let open its sail and fly away.

THE JUSTICE SYSTEM

Sunday is the day the NFL hath made, barbecue and beer logos
in the parking lot accompany an epic skyfall of 100 Russian mothers
dropping in for the halftime show, tangled in parachutes, the whirring
formation of a human snowflake. "The enemy's not poverty,"

Hugo said, "It's wind." Blending, the concussed footballers turn
their grist from end to end, while half the teenagers would sell their
organs to play a single down, or to relieve the mountain of debt that
roars in their sleep. The mascots' giant eyes are unblinking, but their

feisty feet keep them upright beneath the goalposts as their shadows
stab into the field. The raped woman, hiding in full view of the kiss
cam, will manage to forgive her cautious neighbors clinging to their
MP3s, their eyes fixed on the brief history of toilet-based animal

attacks on the Jumbotron, and the ever-growing white comet
of Russians bearing down on the stadium from above. The backup
quarterback is arguing with his coach about the mystery of the American
who woke up speaking Swedish after the lightning strike, awakened

by the sound of himself playing Prokofiev on the piano, having never
played piano, or heard a word of Swedish in his life. "This is what
I'm missing," says the benchwarmer, "the right way to do wrong.
I need to learn to breathe under a mile of mud." In the bleachers

the sludge of chili moving through a million arteries slows the sound
of the marching band as the Russian mothers unlock their fingers and
begin to isolate like geese falling out of their V onto the pillowy lake,
each hardening into a vivid pattern and beginning their improvised descent.

The children pick out the sickles and red stars on the wind-whipped
costumes and think of all the strange spellings in a bowl of alphabet
noodles, and what the clouds must mean, moving aside for the sake
of the show. The cheerleaders' manicured expressions jot upward in

the splintered sunset, alarmed by the sickening variety of colors, and
annoyed by the vendor's hawking song, each plea hoping to make just
one woman stop chewing and see him for the strength of his story,
licking his ration of stamps, as the lights blast open and laser the horizon

and the Russian mothers won't stop falling.

SALVADOR

Laying the cut
                strips of wet cloth
in the noonday sun,
                the saint maker
jerks at a horsefly
                the size of a bullet,
the white plaster
                on his hands spraying
the granite wall
                of the cathedral.

I was called, like everyone else, he says.

He is building a statue
                with chicken wire
and hovers over
                the sidewalk like
a pteradactyl puppet,
                silver hair slicing
the light. When
                they hanged me,
he spouts, I was lost.
                I deserved to die.

I was filled with funny tricks, a braid

of flame was tangled
                    in my backbone.
They were gonna
                    cut my throat, but
everybody wanted
                    to see a hanging,
and there I was.
                    To a hammer,
everything looks
                    like a nail.

When I hit the ground, it took me

            a moment to realize
                    that the rope
had broken and not
                    my neck.
At that point, I was
                    reticent to negotiate,
you understand.
                    I ran into the Father
and he took me in.
                    They have mostly

forgotten the whole thing, by now, and I

still wear the bandage
                    around my neck,
just like the Father
                    does, partly because
he smiles when I
                    point to our collars,
partly to honor
                    the wound that
is everlasting.
                    Who is to say what

force picked me out of the air and plucked

me off that tree
                    like a grape?
I am a fat animal now.
                    I was a frozen sea before,
and the Master
                    handled me with an axe.
In my throat,
                    there is a nest
and it is called
                    The Holy Ghost.

LOOK FOR ME IN LIBERIA

for Nina Simone

What may come
when I sing
Sometimes my voice
is gravel
sometimes
coffee and cream
I splintered
ingested and embraced
Bach
I change keys
right in the middle
Where do I belong?
Wherever the edge is
free from fear

~

All power is black
the ebony squirrels
on the terrace
we ain't made friends
with them yet
Velvet wallpaper
makes the bathroom
feel more blue
Diamonds pasted
on my eyelids
and eyebrows
the balcony of my face

~

The fugue
and counterpoint
makes a high priestess
soul sound
sophisticated
and if they
can't learn to listen
I'll quit
Fuck it
Some dumbass bitch
in the audience
sweating me
I've swallowed the storm
I'll not be rode
I'm a freight train
I tell the track
where to go

~

He beat me
all the way home
Nobody seen me
for two weeks
All the way
in the elevator
up the stairs
He beat me
wham
into a concrete wall
He tells me
I want to be hit
I need it
the scars
he says
to stay straight

~

Everybody knows
about Mississippi
children's brains
scattered
in the sanctuary
Birmingham
and the Bull
got me so upset
bombs in my brain
Selma in my nightgown
goddam
Daddy says
I'm sidetracked
strange fruit
hanging from
the Southern trees
fire hoses opened up
Backlash
is the leather
on this breeze
says Stokely
squeezing
me

~

I'm bathing
in Bloody Marys
addled
and I leave 'em
with the blues
NC backwoods
or cold ass
Carnegie Hall
UNITED SNAKES
OF AMERICA
I want to shake
people free
of their elegant
smugness
and drive
their shriveled hips
insane

~

18,000 students
at the University
of Massachusetts
300 painted black
I quit singing
for anybody else
I want to see
them burn
curious
about themselves
I want to sing
a dagger
into the sick center
of the American soul
I want to cut
the twisted tail
from the world's
largest hog
They don't know
that I'm
already a ghost
wailing descended
backbone
howls

JACK SPICER

Fame is gripped in the fingers
of unctuous, avuncular and
truculent forces, sundries
the promising, demurs in the face
of the wildly authentic and
unorthodox suitor, whose
barbaric insistence is a guarantor
of late commitment, callous
indifference, a posthumous pat
on the corpse's callow head.

BASQUIAT

Unlike Schnabel or Salle
he just didn't have the tools
to negotiate this sea of shit
(and nobody loves a genius child)

I ain't gonna be last year's Negro,
he said, and let slip that sweet smile

Hothouse hybrid
hip graffiti spider
sprawled his cribbed scrawl
showing how obscurity
has its own power

SoHo counter puncher
Venus flytrap shattered by hype
an empath filled with dread

Chic downtown art heroines
still have his dollars tucked
into their stolen Gideon's Bibles

Andy used him and
Madonna used him
and the NY Times
used him and he was
good to the last drop
all his feathers cropped

Another member
with backdoor access
to that horrible artists' guild

Club 27

VILLON

Why look elsewhere,
or scatter the shepherd's
carefully tended fire?
My horse is ribs
and hipbones, too
sore-footed to climb.
The night is a vagabond,
uncertain of its status,
so it thickens and hides
the day's vital trail signs.
I run between windows;
what I can remember
and what is actually
happening, the unforeseen
betrayals, the beeswax
of ordered myths,
holding my fragile
reality intact as it
rolls shiny yellow
in the sweet grass.
How dangerous it is
to dream. Upon what
orders do I murder
the two birds bathing
in the silver river mist
amid the webbing of
my partially frosted mind?

CAPITAL PUNISHMENT

I hate surprises, but I love to be surprised, says the warden.
It's like the difference between Pi the equation, and pie you
can eat. Edified by sudden recognition, whatever you call him,
and it is always, invariably Him, Jesus, Tammuz, Mithra, Krishna,

Attis, Horus, Adonis, even Dionysus, if you please, my feelings
are donkey-faced in the presence of these true believers in reform,
many of whom are landlocked on second shift outposts and can
never understand the evil that men are dying to do. They can only

daydream about their idyllic childhood and the smell of crushed
mint beneath the arched back of their first lover, as the inexhaustible
machines choke down between cigarettes and coffee in the break
area's greasy gossip pits. But here on Death Row, there are no

surprises, each man sits in his single cell, and it's like the lonely
turnpike where one suit fits the only toll booth ticket taker, and
line after line of faceless exhausts churn past inside their dirges.
Random curses split the sounds of metal on metal, or a set

of footsteps reverberating down the freshly mopped hall breaks
the mind's arbitrary focus. The sanguine mourners sing *Kyrie
eleison* as the doctor carefully arranges the syringe mixture.
Three governors and a team of PR execs feed another brown

soul into the media maw. Retarded or whole, the mental challenge
has no seeming moral recourse. We have to prey on the predators
says the governor. We have to win the win, so he buys second
rate pharmaceuticals from Third World countries to quickly put

the animals down. See, they're just sleeping, he muses, as their
hearts wink out. Canceling the light of others is what the prison
does best. On their perches, the crows on the Hill cackle and
caw across the aisle as relations thaw between their black-winged

junior counterparts in the corresponding State House. Pesky DNA
evidence has flipped the switches in the dead of night and the
moratorium storms forward. The hangman isn't hanging, and Old
Sparky has cooked too many convicts in broad daylight, and

popped out their eyeballs in full view of the cameras. Naughty
bits of information bubble out from eyewitness accounts. One
man's skin split like an overcooked hot dog, and his hair caught
fire as he counted down the reasons to stay alive. The black

shackles left slack shadows burned into the dying man's wrists.
The sweetest taboo is the ability to kill without recourse or
remorse, and the complicit public is fed the nefarious details
of the doomed man's crimes and the victims are feted, having

been served the sweet porridge of justice in their own fair time.
Momentum can be deferred, says the social scientists, but it
must always be paid back in full. Silently running through
the Northern towns of America are monsters that will one day

be appointed to lead their tribe's rebellion against the decline
of courtesy and the last vestiges of human decorum before the
locks were picked and the red plague of unseen murders and
mayhem were spread across the campus and the social club.

One false move from the Row, the poorest children learn to handle their business in silence. Beset with oblivion, a being that is drug into the orbits of many planets becomes besotted with the steaming indignities, a world unto themselves, alone

in the seeming complexity, unable to explain the difference.

WRITER'S BLOCK

My head is full of starts and stops,
wind in my teeth and curses
disguised as words in my ears,
cavities of dreams jumbled between.

When the doctors
opened their patients
they found landscapes,
beaches, mountains, skies.

What are the names of the angels
and the birds? My memories swarm
round like confused flies. Among
the dead, I cherish most myself.

RUNNING WITH THE BULLS

in memory of Manolete

Tightly strung, like the neck of a guitar,
dancing with a ton of charred fury,
a matador does not slouch or feint,
or couch his gestures to the gallery
with satirical intent. The Beast

does not repeat its mistakes
until its enemy, a jeweled reed
in the wind, is in full focus,
popping out of the cushion of his cape
like a pin, his doomed eyes
shaded with delirium.

In love with Death, or so it seemed,
wise flies' black buzz streaming over his life
like the high tide's meticulous fuzz,
gored and awash in blood,
the storm's pageantry pushed him

out past the breaking point,
his prayers replaced by the sound of wings,
in love with the rent fabric of his own singing,
the reef snapping off the wave's soft seam,
holding his broken body aloft

as the sky filled with bloody petals,
riddling his coffin with red hail,
three days of dirges and his salty animal's
swollen blue smell, weightless
in the swirling mania,
running with the bulls.

CEREMONY

You can't stand on it
or be dumped by it, un
ceremoniously, or other
wise. It's the bid-rigging

that makes you want to
find your own starlet,
oozily boozy and wildly
willing to succumb to

the dealer and the middle
of his fourth shoe, though
if you ever make a real
run in Vegas, or Hollywood,

then all bets are off, life
won't lay the same way
again and the definitions
of your previous scandals

are formidably challenged
and secretly downgraded,
changed as it were, in the
light of fresh circumstances.

Take Terrorism, for example,
which was once defined
by the Oxford English Dictionary
as *government by intimidation,*

and now whole governments
are intimidated by a handful
of foreign terrorists with their
mind on paradise and their

fingertips sliding greasily
over the uncertain construction
of their underwear bomb.
It takes a village idiot to

kill them softly, with sordid
reviews and bad word of mouth.
The English invented football,
what we roughnecks call soccer,

when they kicked around
the heads of Danish invaders
they had slaughtered. And that's
where the whole mess gets tricky,

you see, one man's game is the
other's life in full, with the power
of luck attesting to the difference
between a top and a bottom.

In ten minutes a hurricane
releases more energy than
all the world's nuclear
weapons detonated at once.

That puts the eye on that
particular apocalypse trigger
in several places at the same
time, and we're already running

out of names for our hurricanes.
There are more plastic flamingoes
than real ones in the United States,
but all the swans in England

are property of the Queen;
just the mention of a public
superstition, for instance,
that the mad, pacing ravens

kept in the Tower of London,
would cause the monarchy to fail
if they were ever to leave,
creates a job for a British citizen,

someone to clip the raven's wings
assuring that they stay put.
Drones in a hive have only
one job, to mate with

their Queen, and those lucky
enough to do so, die in the act.
It is a tender fact that the heart
of a full-grown blue whale

is as large as a small Toyota,
and its tongue is as long as an
elephant, tail to trunk, but
when the dealer spies a whale,

the casino is alerted and his
chances get the swell swatted
right out of them. It ain't the love
that gets you killed, it's the letter,

not the spike that wins the point,
it's the setter, the machinations
of the tapping shoes, accompanied
by piano, go tipping down the

wrong dark alley, just to help
a friend; or you hear the rhythm
in the square and for a second,
bending to listen, step off

in front of the onrushing bus,
whose passengers' mortified
eyes reveal your fresh future,
and its brakes announce your

                    end.

DEAR READER

When our bodies merge
there is a sanctuary
where all the ghosts
of our gathered past
assemble to worship
and in order for our
minds to find the way
they set themselves
                on fire

HOUDINI AND THE DEAD LETTER OFFICE

Houdini made a five-ton elephant
disappear before five thousand
people at the Hippodrome Theater
in New York City and stared down
two mystics as he darted between
trotting police horses at the south
east corner of Sixth Avenue proper.
Handcuffed underwater with a pick
in his cheek, the rats on the wharf,
whose whiskers tensed as he swam,
cowered in their fur as he emerged.
His shivery, freshly rinsed skin, even
slathered with the slurred, whiskey
thick sentences of the society lips and
subsequent licks of repentance, was
still as resistant to bursting in bloom
as it had always been. Some early
misfortune had embittered his life.
When Harry entered the dead letter
office, he sensed the stories that lay
dormant in the must, the place where
all the disappeared things in the world
went to find their file, the large shadow
of his elephant crept quietly across
the wall, its delicate ears wafting like
the wings of a shy angel. Houdini smiled
as he watched it fly. Weightless dust
motes riding mini thermals followed
his footsteps among the drifting
mountains of lost names. Nothing stays

where you put it, and the trick is not to let
the disappeared thing stay away too long.
Trilliums of frosted voices scattered
like elisions among the catacombs
of filing cabinets, kings on their broken
thrones moaned through the corridors
for their coterie of forgotten servants,
misplaced notes unopened, undelivered
pleas and kingdoms, like glacial erratics,
were orphaned by the entry to another
gloomy cul de sac. The hedges that form
the labyrinth surrounding the windows
grew unruly, and Houdini coughed out
the key to the hidden cabinet and palmed
it as he passed the astronomers without
borders blowing out of the upper drawers
of redrawn maps and surveys overwhelmed
with statistical errors, clouds of stars whose
names were squirreled away with their
subjects' black implosion. Harry assumed
through his magic that all things are in
contact and he blew into his fingers the
warm current that sent the key like an arrow
to its lock. Ptolemy's voice creaked and
the room went berserk with bronze silence.
Houdini's elephant giggled and flew back
into the wall. Forty burning monks,
with their shaved heads, sat lotus forming
a mandala and Harry slivered in, seeing
the entire hall from the light of their meteor.

Mummies, loosed from their tombs,
wandered blindly past, ribbons of their
bodies unraveling. The confetti of burned
Mayan texts and medieval incantations
leapt off their scrolls and wrapped round
the empty space where Houdini had just left
and deftly placed his ear against the silk
membrane of an ancient Chinese backdrop
constructed for a play forgotten by its poet.
The elephant's rump bulged from the other
side and Harry smoothed his hands
on the outline of its tail and pulled
with all his might. Blinded by the footlights
for a split second, the master stood up,
stiff wand shining in his hand, as the
applause washed over him in the grand
Hippodrome, five thousand throats roaring
with wonder, as Houdini, still angry
with his pet, turned with a resigned sigh
and bowed for the drunken crowd.

LE PAPILLON

This is not the righteous blue flame that engulfs the monk,
or the sherbet agent of invisible acid dropped by the barrel
on the naked children of starving villages in South Vietnam,
not the 80 proof orange vodka cocktail lit by the free-basing
Richard Pryor, a black adder, addled by self-loathing, who
poured the fire over his head, and ran screaming into the void.
This is not the match strike under the cooking spoonful, any
more than it is the convulsive propulsion shivering into
massive tendrils that annihilate the bloated Hindenburg
in an avalanche of star-like implosion, a fire that blotted out
a flying cathedral between its fingers.

no

This is the personal
and public incineration snapping its jaws shut around the
most delicate jubilant wings. This is the interrupted gravity-
free white lance that burns straight through the curtain,
the laser emitted by a magnifying glass as it focuses a ray
of the sun on an unsuspecting dragonfly, the wisp of smoke,
almost a held breath of frost let slowly out, then the shards
red and jagged, slicing through the tutu's layers and igniting
them, delicate as tissue paper sticking to the ballerina's hips
as she twisted away from the guilty footlights and swarmed
into the backstage, a thousand ingots of red and lavender
knives exploding around her supple hands and shoulders,
a galaxy of bees hiving her, a flare, a comet, and finally
a nest of ash, hoping to hold together in the wind.

DEATH TREK

With Time bearing down,
beating its wings of rusty blades,
how many broken lives do we get?

Swinging by our feet,
we embrace the days of the dead
drinking the sky's ashes
from a hardened gourd,

sharing a mug of rum
in the ramshackle cemetery
with all the old uncles.

St. James pinches rain
from the eyes of the gods
and kisses the cinnamon lips
of long dead idols

as tree limbs creak
and the jungle collapses
underneath the weight
of its great soggy cargo.

Chiles, tomatoes, corn and beans
rode their cactus steeds
across the civilized markets.

My head is full of stars,
wind in my teeth
and dreams jumbled between
the white noise
of a million birds.

My memories swarm round
like confused flies.
We unravel as we travel, but
the dismembered dead remain.

~

Air, earth, fire and water
herald the floating world
and tangle their tail feathers
in the green coffee groves.

Large globes of dazzling light
remind the warped gourds
of their golden age,

and the skull's still life
of yellow and blue angels
is emptied of its threshold
with the brain alone in its stew.

What I sought to circle
derives its form from flight,
my interior flooded,

fluttering with violins,
and every open window

was filled with the space
a song makes,
the frequent muscle mystery
of lavender notes

and long flowing lines,
the motion of music
as it flutters through the mind.

Among the snarling gardens,
at the edge of the high sierras,
I was warned to
trust the teller and not the tale.

The human capacity
for gratitude is limited
by the presence of the dead.

~

Inside the gratitude is envy,
says the priest.
Inside the envy
is the indifference
of a heedless village,

and yet as my senses filled
with wild mountain oregano
and lush blueberry wine

the sisters were hushed
spinning wool
on their single spools
and weaving belts and serapes
on their waist looms

favoring their hips
in the balance
of their black skirts
and shaping a clay pot
with a corn cob

offering a broken melon
with a wooden spoon
and honey-flavored pulka
from a plucked cactus

and the demons
in the web of death
were struck dumb
and learned to live broken,
sitting quietly on their hands.

It takes two days
to celebrate a dead child
the solemn sisters said.

~

Below the volcano
the San Pedro church
heralds the traffic fatalities
with a trail of yellow marigolds.

The vendors
and the catacombs uncoil
as one pyramid
set to boil
swallows the next

and a hundred varieties
of hot chiles are stuffed
into turkey frijoles
and oblong sheep intestines,

blue corn quesadillas
and fried tomato fritters,
onions shining on their skin
like studded diamonds.

The poor in Puebla love Raphael
and watch grinning skeletons
parade arm in arm
below window sills
shocked shivery with candlelight.

Crushed beetles
make the red paint pop
and add their holy dimension
to the backdrop
of tear-stained skulls.

The dead are sad
because they can no longer eat
and cherish the dents
in the domesticated apple,

the stains on the chicken breast
slathered in chocolate sauce,
with pumpkin and garlic
riding on the spiced guacamole.

~

Every laughing ancestor
knows their way to the altar
and follow the scent
of sausage patties
curing among the smoke
of pine-scented incense.

Seasoned grasshoppers soaking
in lime juice wait patiently
among the tacos and hominy

as the names of the dead
are softly repeated,
a communion of the living
and the freshly departed.

The wizened grandfather,
with a satchel of sugar loaves,
is prepared for their visit,
crosses himself with a pistol
and uses its hammer
to untie the loose knot
that holds the bread together

and fires a shot into the sapling
at the edge of the proceedings,
his blunt bullet lodged
in the tree's slender waist,

above the last open grave
that is punctuated
in its open face
with a firework clutch of lime

like a swollen white
carnation blossom
on a fire-blackened field,

where death has become
God's medicine for the desert
and everyone
is slowly bathing in it.

BUILDING A CIRCUS ON
THE SOUND OF WINGS

If I was flying through the air,
as the city laid out its tiny lights
and perfect corners like pins
on a grid, your opinion would not
matter, with the weight of the wind
beneath me and wisps of clouds
separating into vapor, revealed
in the vast sky to be nothing
but water changing its mind.

Feeble, inaccessible, we think
we're following the voices of angels,
experts without experience,
whose elastic vanity never
allows the music to falter,
whose blood has never been wasted,
forgetting it is the essential business
of being human, this stumbling around.

And you are easily rattled,
your decision to collect slights
and hold them like shells in a bag,
injured by the ringing in a stew of voices,
each inadvertent sting denting your crown,
the lines dragged across your brow,
resembles a field full of arrowheads,
freshly plowed—

It is easy for conflict to find us,
and that's what makes us clumsy,
the absence of pleasure,
and our love of its brevity,
already derided and defeated,
with nothing further to lose,
we hurry to plunge our blunt tools
into the nearest man or beast.

And when you bite my cheek,
or hold my voice underwater,
your performance is not murder,
but the prestige of the theatre,
like a passenger balloon revealed to be
a tarp when all the air escapes, and as it
rushes, creates a growing inertia, like riding
a bicycle with no hands off the end of the pier.

The boulder that is growing
inside you is nourished by
the perceived slights of passersby,
when your fingers are blackened
by newsprint, and ink blots are
transforming into monsters,
nodding their heads in tacit agreements
that only you can see. When you walk,
you can feel your bones moving.

The spiders, dragonflies, and slugs
are savage, sensing the nests in
your hysteria. Torpedoes of trout race
haphazardly back and forth,
intent on chaos, swallowing flies
like grains of gunpowder and scratching
the fuses of their fins against the rocks.
The hats are ridiculous, holding people
by their heads against the ground.

This weight that no one can relinquish,
so many voices, growing in volume,
create by their discordant patterns
a kind of music, like overlapping waves
that scratch apart the beach,
stories bent on their own annihilation,
confirming that one cannot make a life
of passing glances, or the lack thereof,
or a circus from the sound of wings.

THE MOUNTAIN THAT EATS MEN

forced into a seam
the grace of the play
is its animal pulse

  I thread my breath
and the shale walls frost
the first edge of the world's
ruin creeps into view

the shallow greedy water
shimmering in our boot tracks
reflects every moon thin
crack of light or match strike
to light a cigarette or another
  belch of dynamite

as the musicians
blindfolded in a beige room
filled with dreams of peacocks
make their strings mew
  like frightened birds

plucking the cat gut
stretched tight and dig out
chunks of the darkness
between their fingers

Jimmy's broken back
was eerily silent
like the spine of a book
bent too far and
its fibers splitting

    as the smoke thickened
and all the choirs in my body
sang their false notes
one against the other

like a sword thrust into a mirror
each piece destroying the harmony
of my blood's black symmetry

    the aisles betray the balcony
as the columns forget their lines
and turn away in embarrassment

    their windows shuttered
as the cracked vessels
in my shipwrecked eyes
covered in streaks of lightning

    lay down like stars
on the windowsill
of a darkening waterfall
      and slowly fall apart

conspiring with the scenery
to destroy the play
clouds of whales covered the sun
with their flumes and outstretched tails
drowned beneath these barges

I was swamped and alone
in a jagged blind avalanche
of freshly baptized sounds

glyphs lift from their pyramids
and serve as seconds
for the insomniacs and hidden frescoes

dueling at twenty paces
with loaded gondolas of coal

ANTIETAM

whispering armies and the swish of cornstalks
as they brushed across the rough blood-streaked
uniforms and the dull glare of Confederate fires
the only glow behind the receding hillside in its
indigo twilight punctured by the occasional curse
of a soldier stumbling over another body or the
terrified hump of a dog lost inside the labyrinth
of undulating lines three hundred yards apart in
rectangles of armories backed against the quietly
rolling Potomac and as the sun rose nine thousand
came boiling from the black woods toward the old
hulk of Dunker Church the glamour of their shiny
bayonets polished to separate a man from his long
held convictions though the barrage of sharp balls
barked from the corn and beat divots in that double
time charge and those that did not fall in the fresh
morning light rolled onward loading and cursing
as they dodged the fallen screeching hysterically
and advanced into the teeth of a monster they had
long feared but had not fed steel whizzing like mad
hornets past their lowered heads and all the generals
present cried forward and pushed Hood and Lee and
Stonewall then McClellan and Hooker and Burnside
skulls cracked like eggshells and shots lodged in tree
after tree the taste of uncooked coffee grounds stuck
in their gritted teeth and gunpowder caking their lips
even those that were ordered to retreat met their fate
as they climbed the split rail fence and hung there
like wrinkled laundry in its stakes as Longstreet's
brave Georgians faced the humpbacked bridge and

held their opponents for three hours before they
broke and splashed face first in the teeming creek
new recruits lay in the wagon tracks of the Sunken
Road picking off the silhouetted heads of the blind
sided Union men riding ragged horses across the
steep bluff their hats in comic relief against the sky
for the love of God uttered one rookie with both
eyes shot out and his lieutenant obliged before a
cannon obliterated even this merciful act and took
the commander's head away and Clara Barton felt
the Lord tug her sleeve only to find a bullet had
pierced her dress and nested in the face of the poor
soldier she held and she looked down the lane to
see the broken bodies like cobblestones laid neatly
in rows stretching away toward the Capitol Domes
before the muskets growled again and the armies
clawed toward Sharpsburg where future presidents
McKinley and Hayes discussed their last biscuits
and watched as General Hill waded in with his red
shirt from Harper's Ferry allowing Lee to claim his
hold on the shattered field before he crept away in
bruised darkness southward counting the massive
amounts of lost souls and then the click of Brady's
black cameras which slowly shuddered at the
reflected pyramids of dead dueling in the borders
with the laughs of scarred ecstatic crows bowing
and pecking in a gluttonous rush for the scraps

COFFIN NOT INCLUDED

Gradually the world shuts you out,
your plum skin dapples and craters,
effectively exhausted by holding back
the waterfall that is a human being.
There is no getting used to sorrow;
every encounter, like the rungs of a ladder
lap higher and harder until the rails
turn to eels in your hands and escape
as ropes of smoke, weary of the body
and its constant demands. The walls
between this world and the next
are leaky as an old rowboat.
Heated commerce passes between them,
a musical wind, ribbons of distress
wound into our bones by ghosts.
Music can pass for conversation,
says things not entirely human,
beyond the realm of words, notes
hanging on their wires like unruffled birds.
How we are usually complicit in
the things we complain about, and yet
we have so little control over what we create.
Music makes me do just what it wants me to.
Furry arroyos, full of cactus shadows,
know that among the holies,
there is more than one ghost.

THE SILVER SURFER

for Stan Lee

A froth of moon reveals
the hissing river,
                    momentarily
pausing
        for the silver owl
to drop
        on a rabbit and
orchestrate its death curdle.

The roof,
        bathed in a creamy glow,
seems covered in snow,
                    but it is
late August and the white trees
in the waning moonlight
                    are resolute
against the black curtain.
                    The sky
is burning,
        released from its burden,
to buoy
        on its fingertips,
the mythology of a perfect night.

The suicides,
                    convinced it is so,
open their veins, step off
                              the building,
or drink down
                    a Milky Way of valium,
each star
          they swallow
                         flooding
their skull with light.
                         I save what I can,
riding the crest of ever-
                         collapsing darkness,
trying to catch
                    the unbroken bodies
                         in my arms.

BIOGRAPHICAL NOTE

Keith Flynn (www.keithflynn.net) is the award-winning author of seven books, most recently *Colony Collapse Disorder* (Wings Press, 2013) and a collection of essays entitled *The Rhythm Method, Razzmatazz and Memory: How to Make Your Poetry Swing* (Writer's Digest Books, 2007). From 1984–1999, he was the lyricist and lead singer for the nationally acclaimed rock band The Crystal Zoo, which produced three albums: *Swimming Through Lake Eerie* (1992), *Pouch* (1996), and the spoken word and music compilation *Nervous Splendor* (2003). He is currently touring with a supporting combo, The Holy Men, whose album, *LIVE at Diana Wortham Theatre*, was released in 2011. He is the Executive Director and producer of the TV show *LIVE at White Rock Hall* and of Animal Sounds Productions, both of which create collaborations between writers and musicians in video and audio formats. His award-winning poetry and essays have appeared in many journals and anthologies around the world, including the *American Literary Review*, the *Colorado Review*, *Poetry Wales*, *Five Points*, *Poetry East*, the *Southern Poetry Anthology*, the *Poetics of American Song Lyrics*, *Writer's Chronicle*, the *Cimarron Review*, *Rattle*, *Shenandoah*, *Word and Witness: 100 Years of North Carolina Poetry*, *Crazyhorse*, and many others. He has been awarded the Sandburg Prize for poetry, a 2013 North Carolina Literary Fellowship, the ASCAP Emerging Songwriter Prize, the Paumanok Poetry Award, and was twice named the Gilbert-Chappell Distinguished Poet for North Carolina. Flynn is the founder and managing editor of the *Asheville Poetry Review*, which began publishing in 1994.